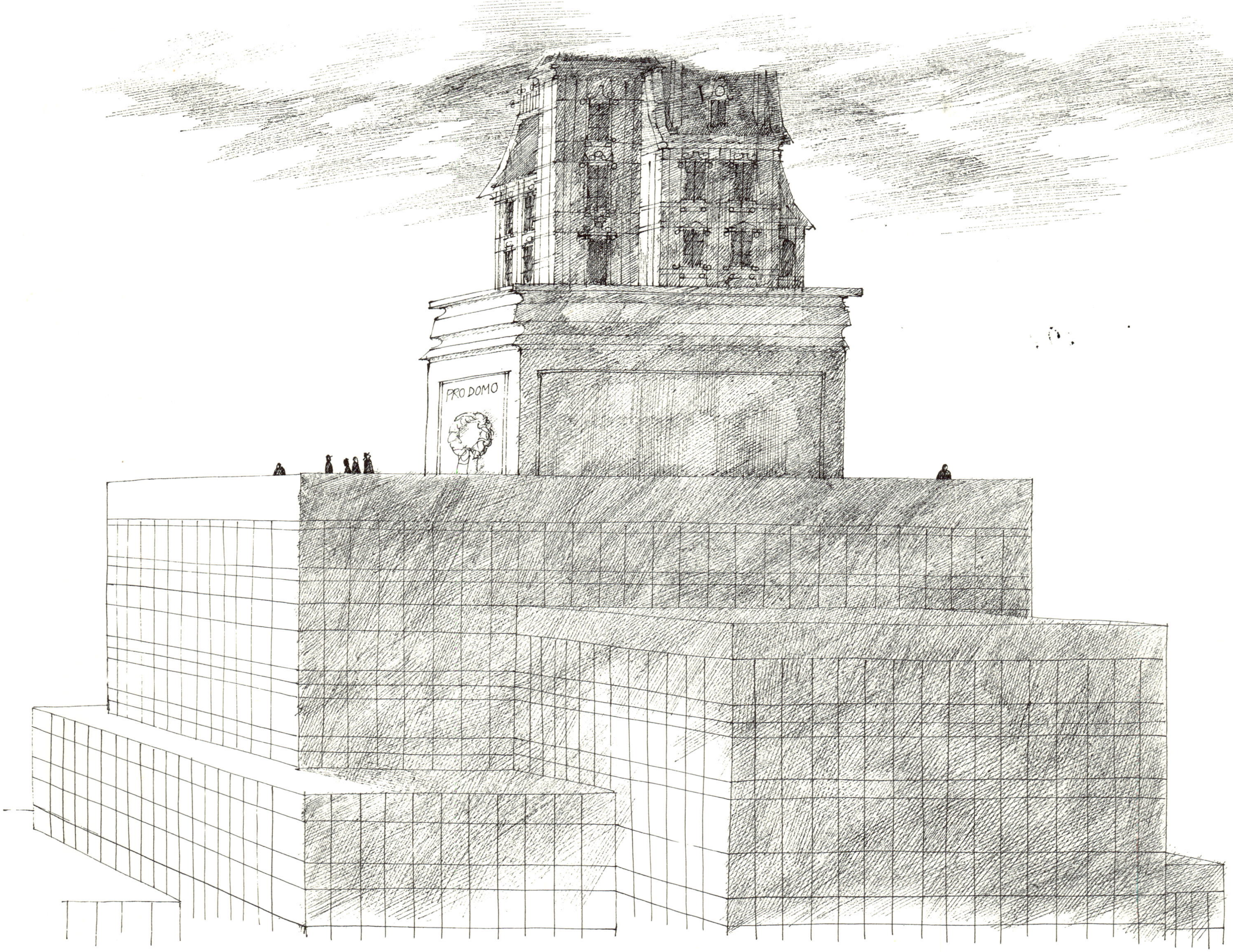
PRO DOMO

PAUL FLORA
PENTHOUSE

HARRY N. ABRAMS, INC., PUBLISHERS, NEW YORK

Jacket illustration: HOTEL DES ALPES I. 1976
Frontispiece: MEMORIAL FOR A HOUSE. 1976

Library of Congress Catalog Card Number: 78-73630
International Standard Book Number: 0-8109-2163-4

Published in 1978 by Harry N. Abrams, Incorporated, New York
Copyright 1977 in Switzerland by Diogenes Verlag AG, Zurich
All rights reserved. No part of the contents of this book
may be reproduced without the written permission of the publishers

Printed and bound in the United States of America

house, n. a hollow edifice erected for the habitation of man, rat, mouse, beetle, cockroach, fly, mosquito, flea, bacillus and microbe.

AMBROSE BIERCE, *The Devil's Dictionary*

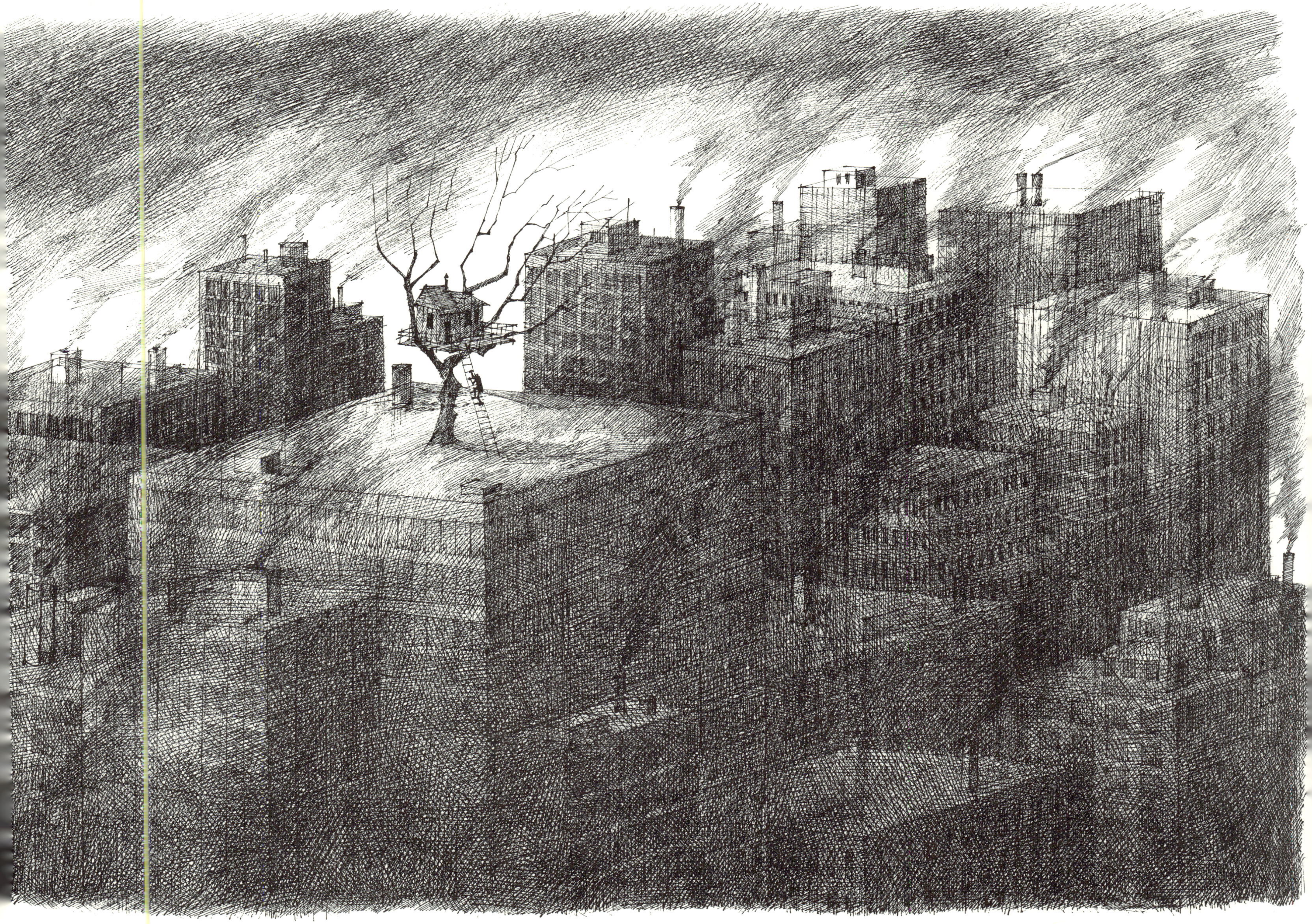

AN ESCAPIST. 1975

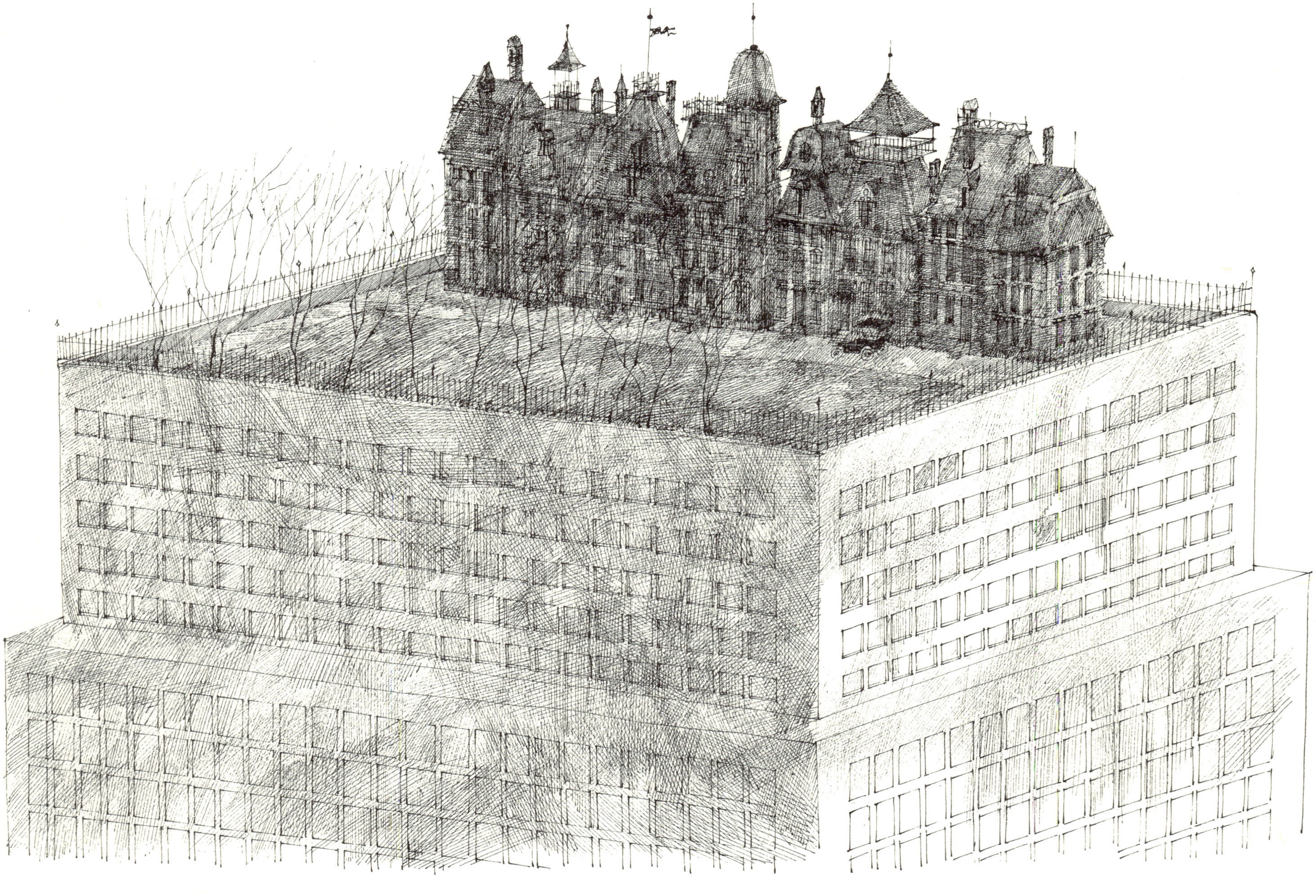

FORD T 8. 1974

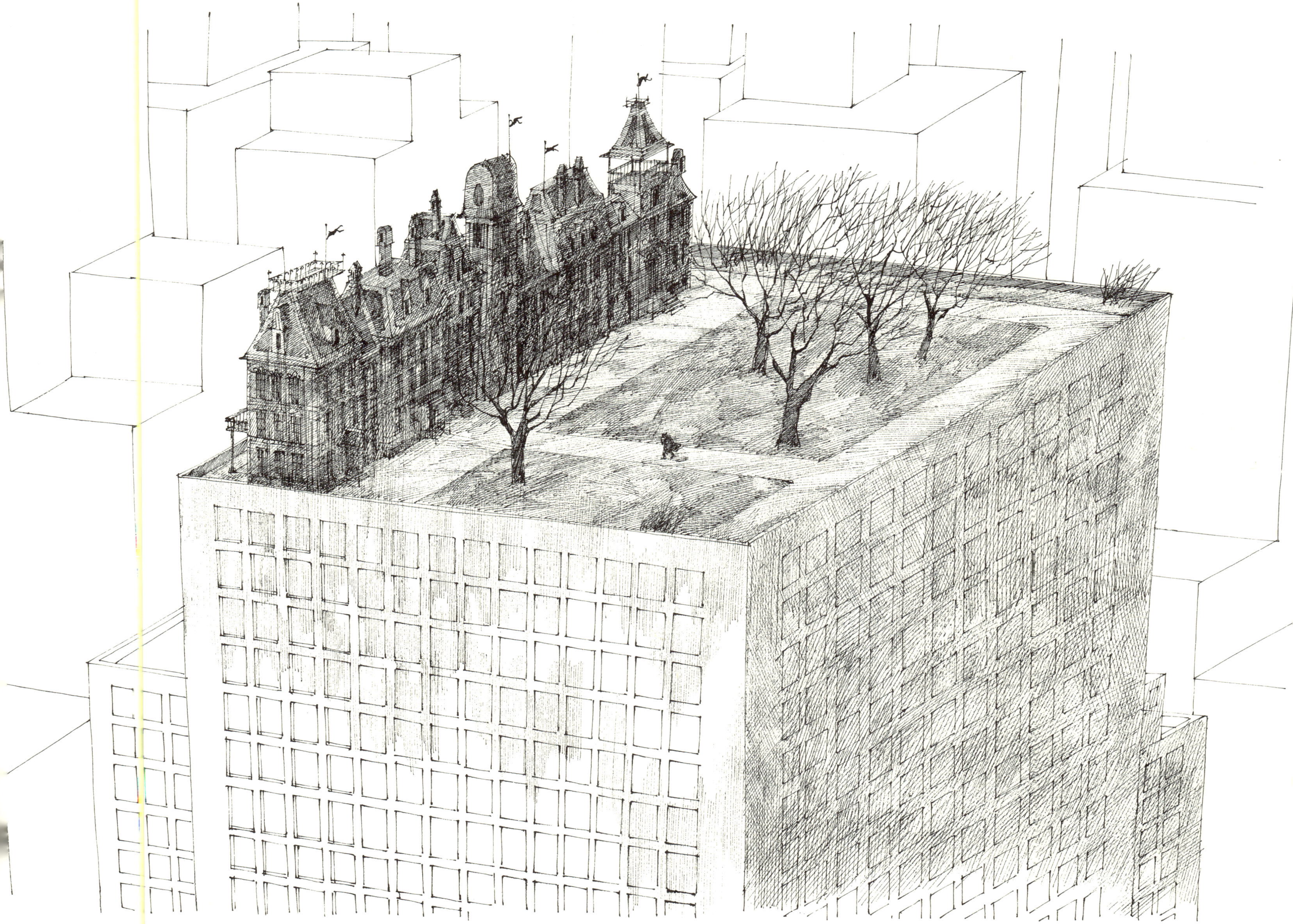

THE WANDERER. 1974

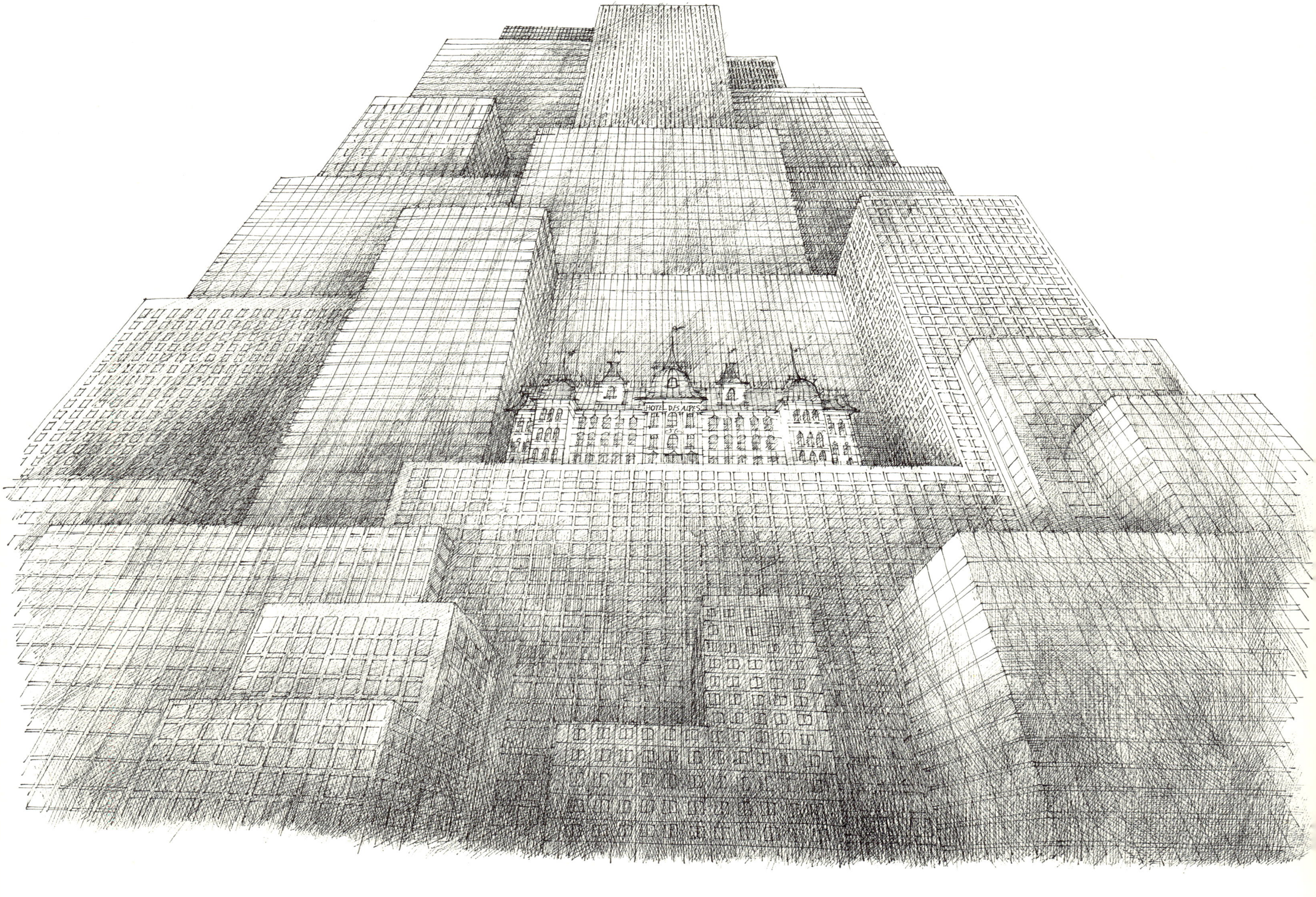
HOTEL DES ALPES

HOTEL DES ALPES II. 1977

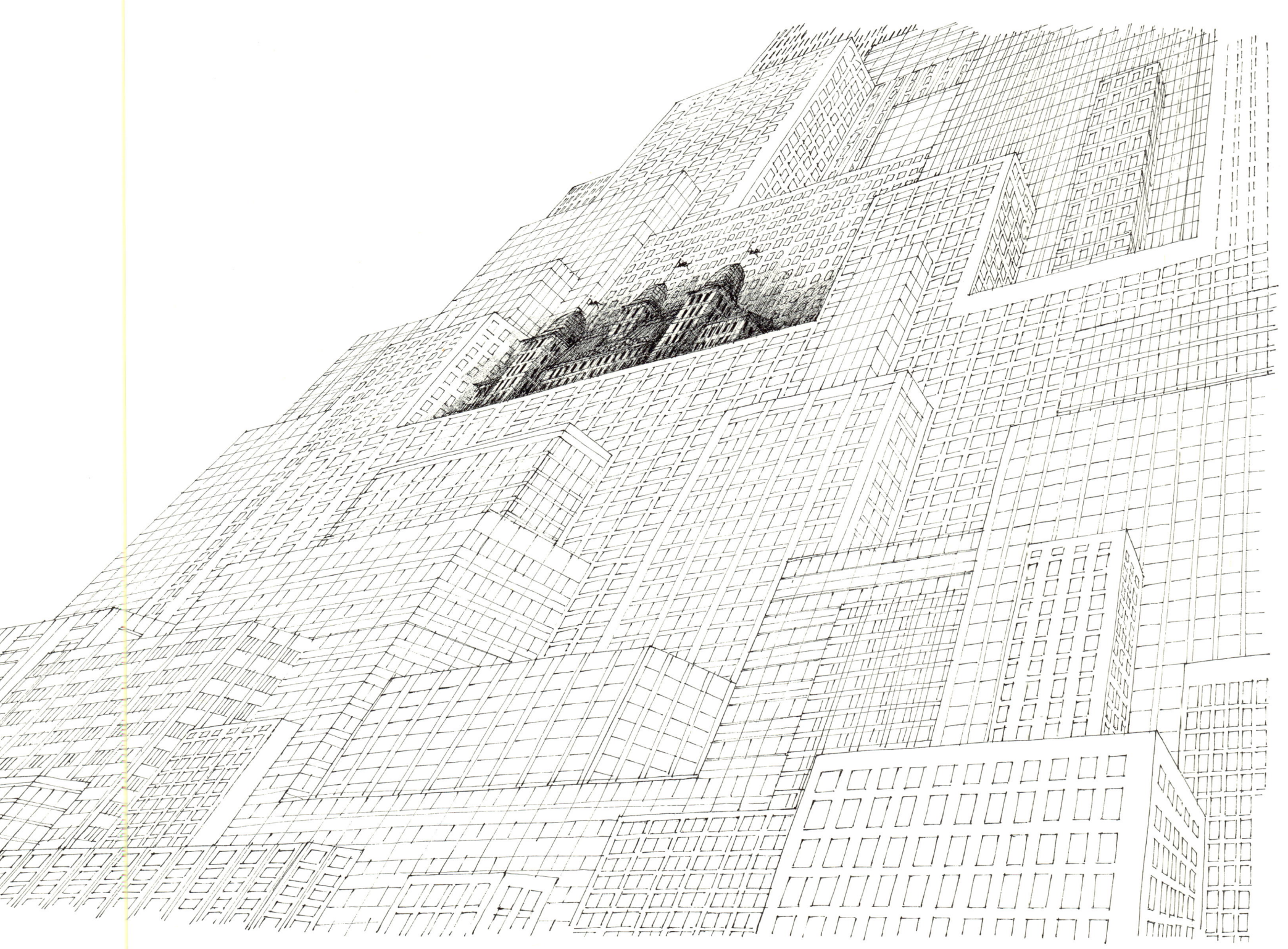

HOTEL DES ALPES III. 1977

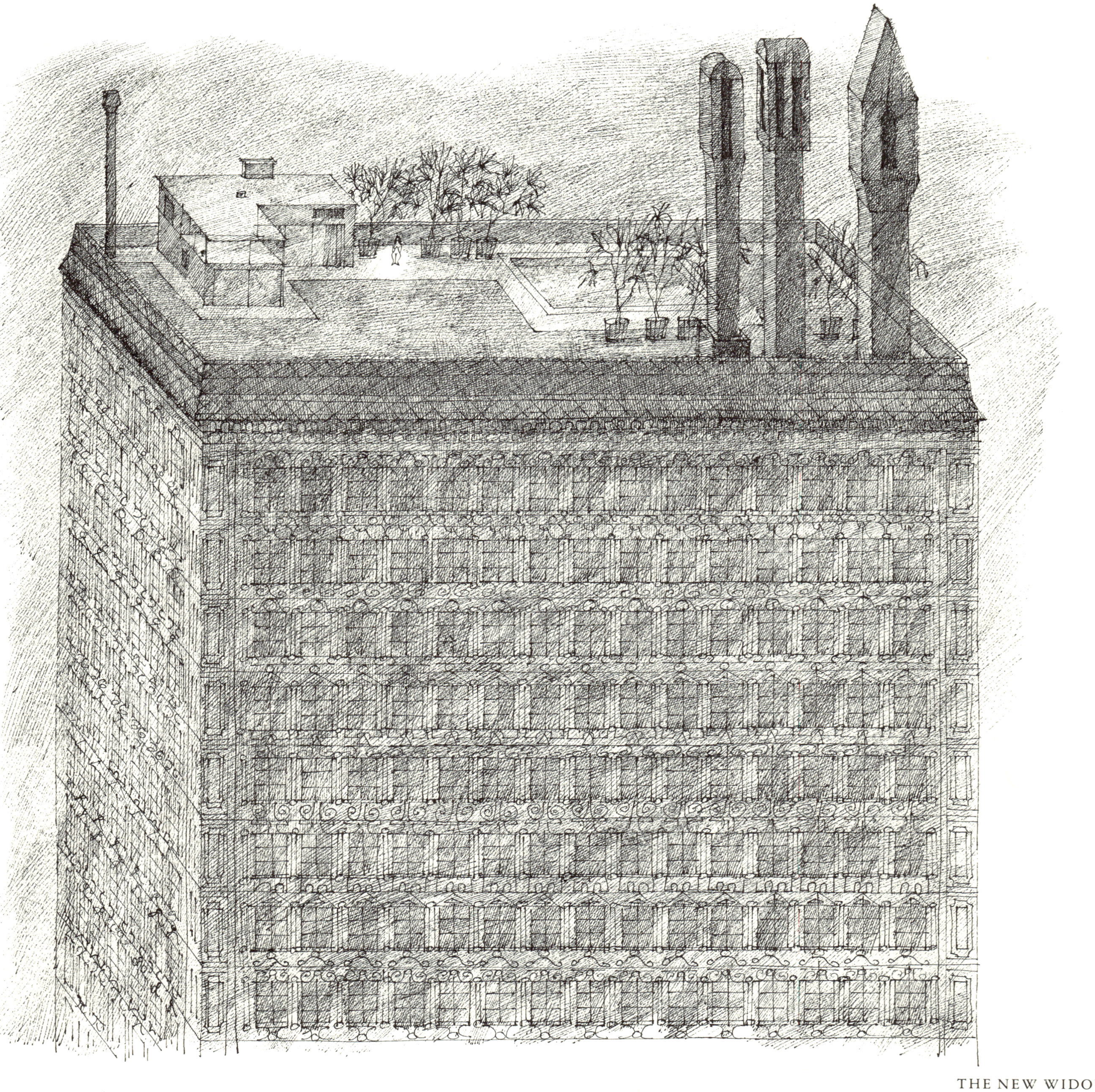

THE NEW WIDOW. 1976

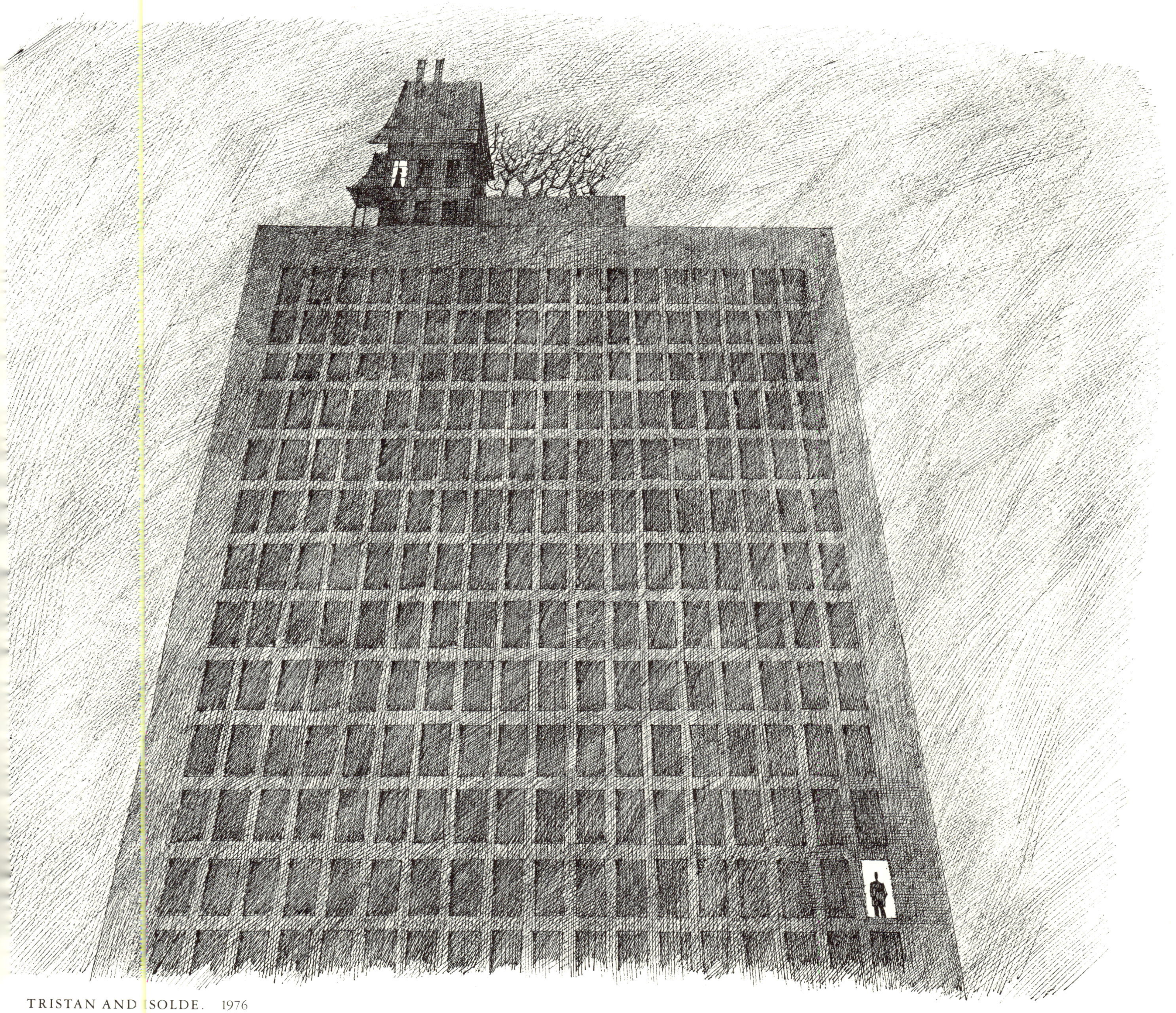

TRISTAN AND ISOLDE. 1976

IN MARCH. 1976

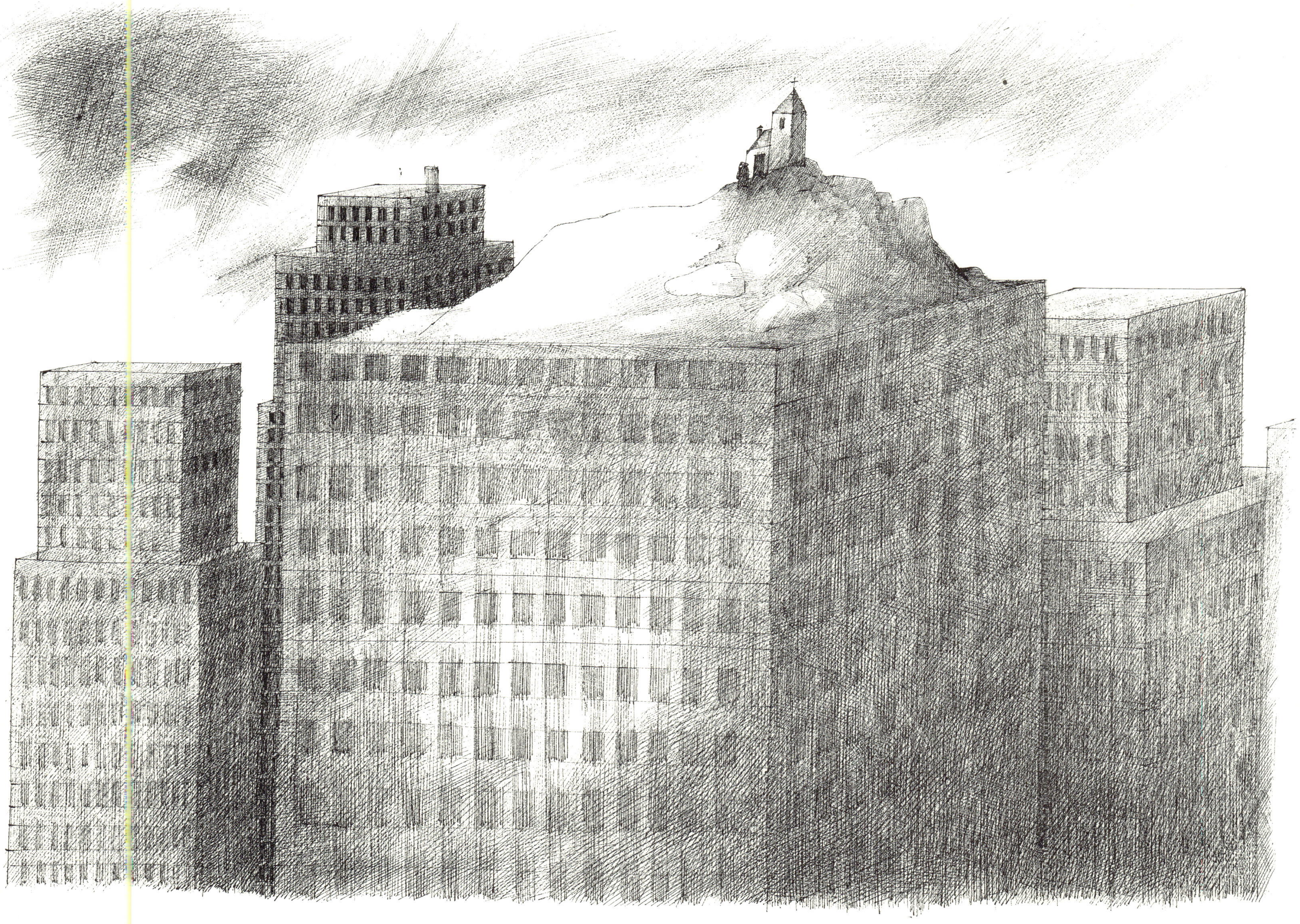

THE HERMIT. 1974

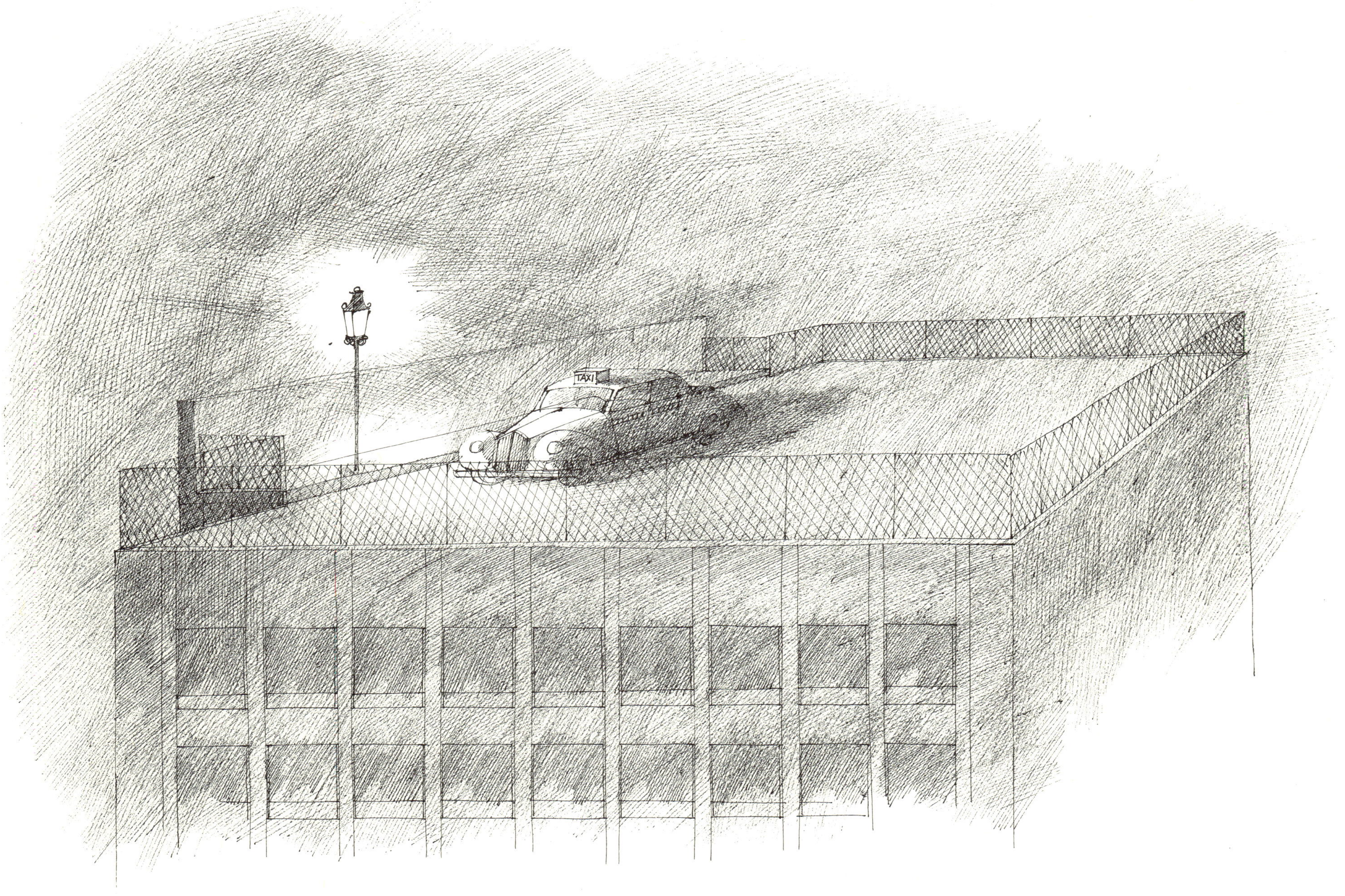
TAXI

WAITING. 1976

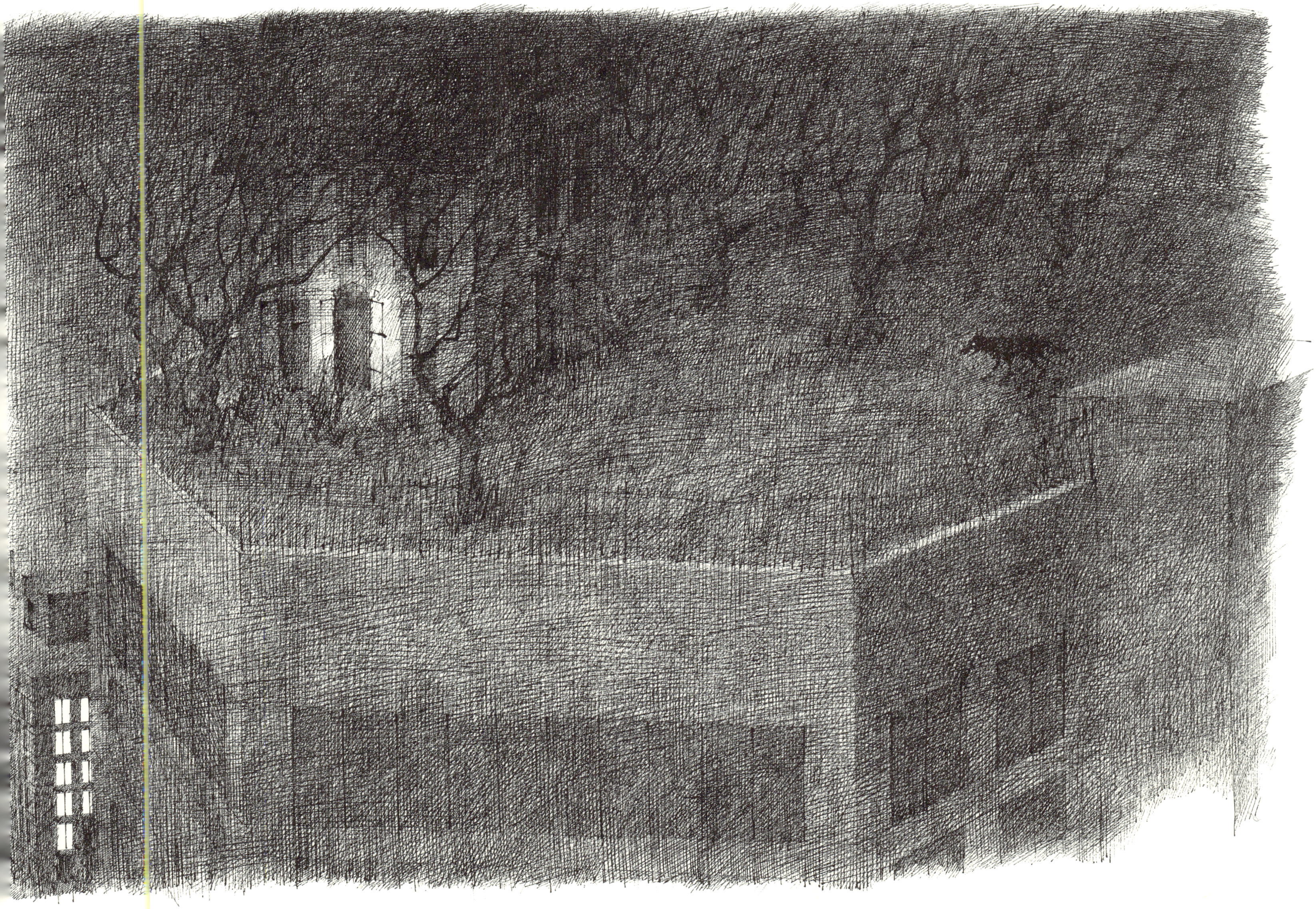

AN ABANDONED PLACE. 1976

ASYLUM FOR DRUNKARDS. 1976

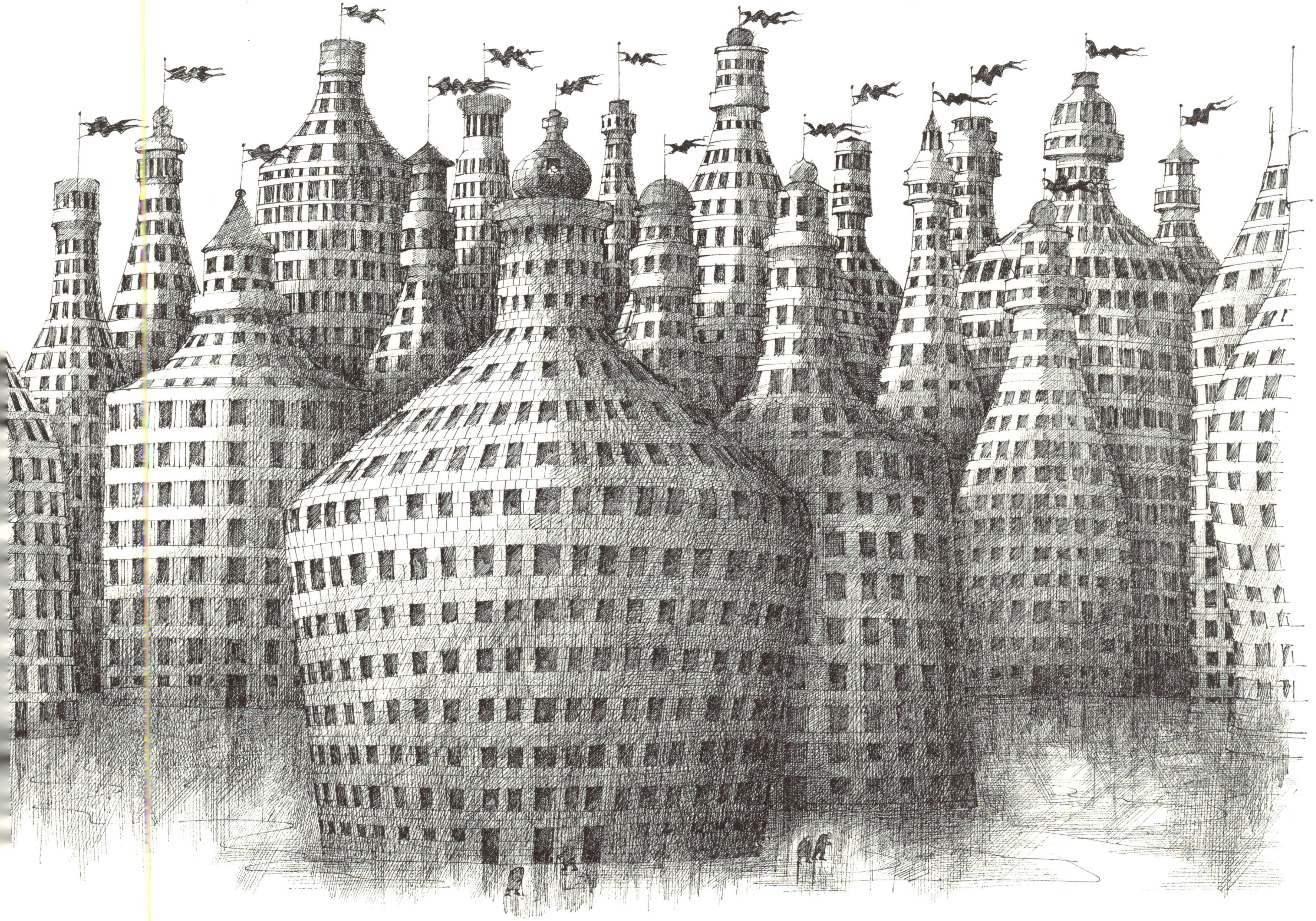

DRUNKARDS' CITY. 1976

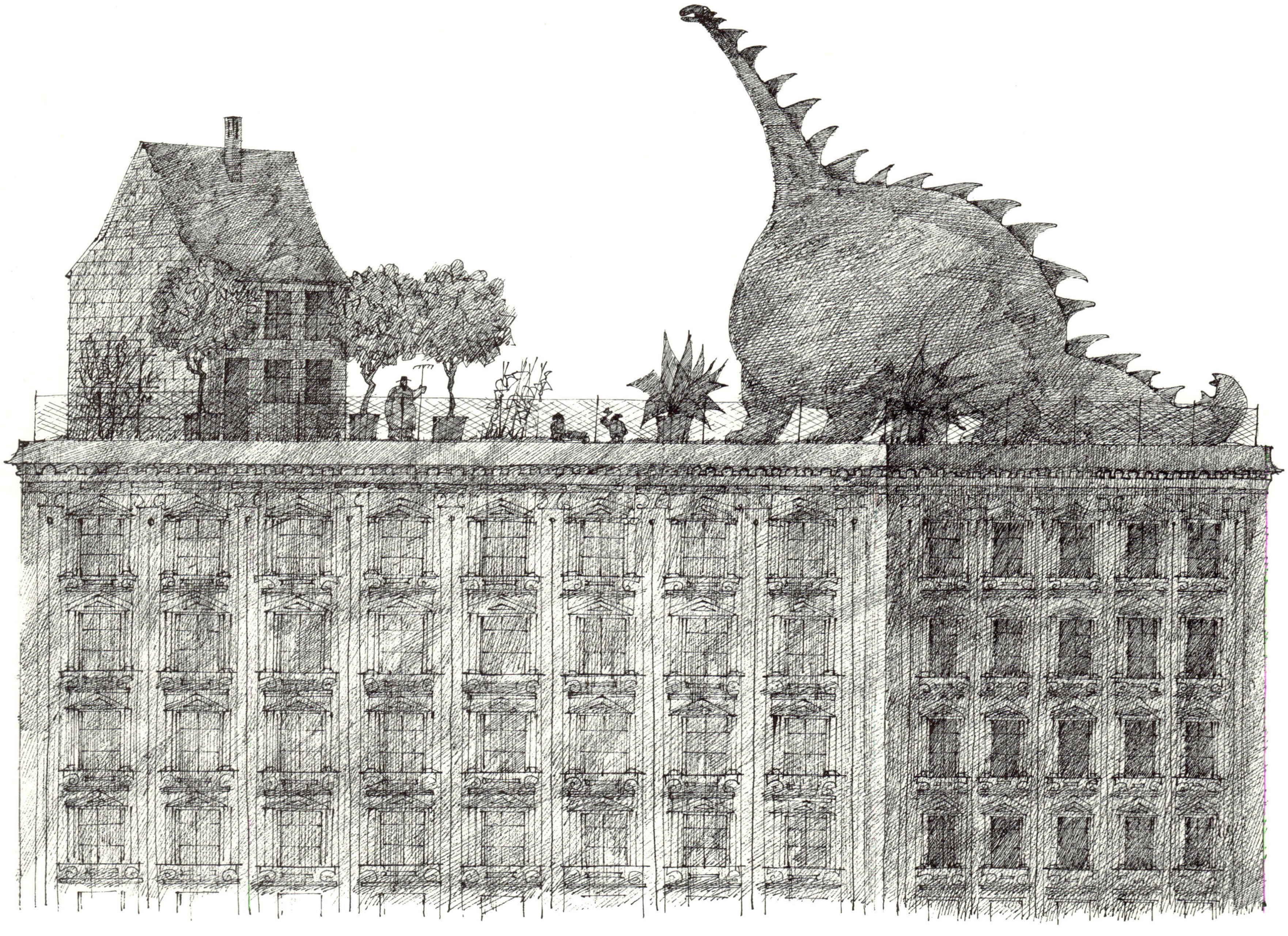

SMALLHOLDING I. 1976

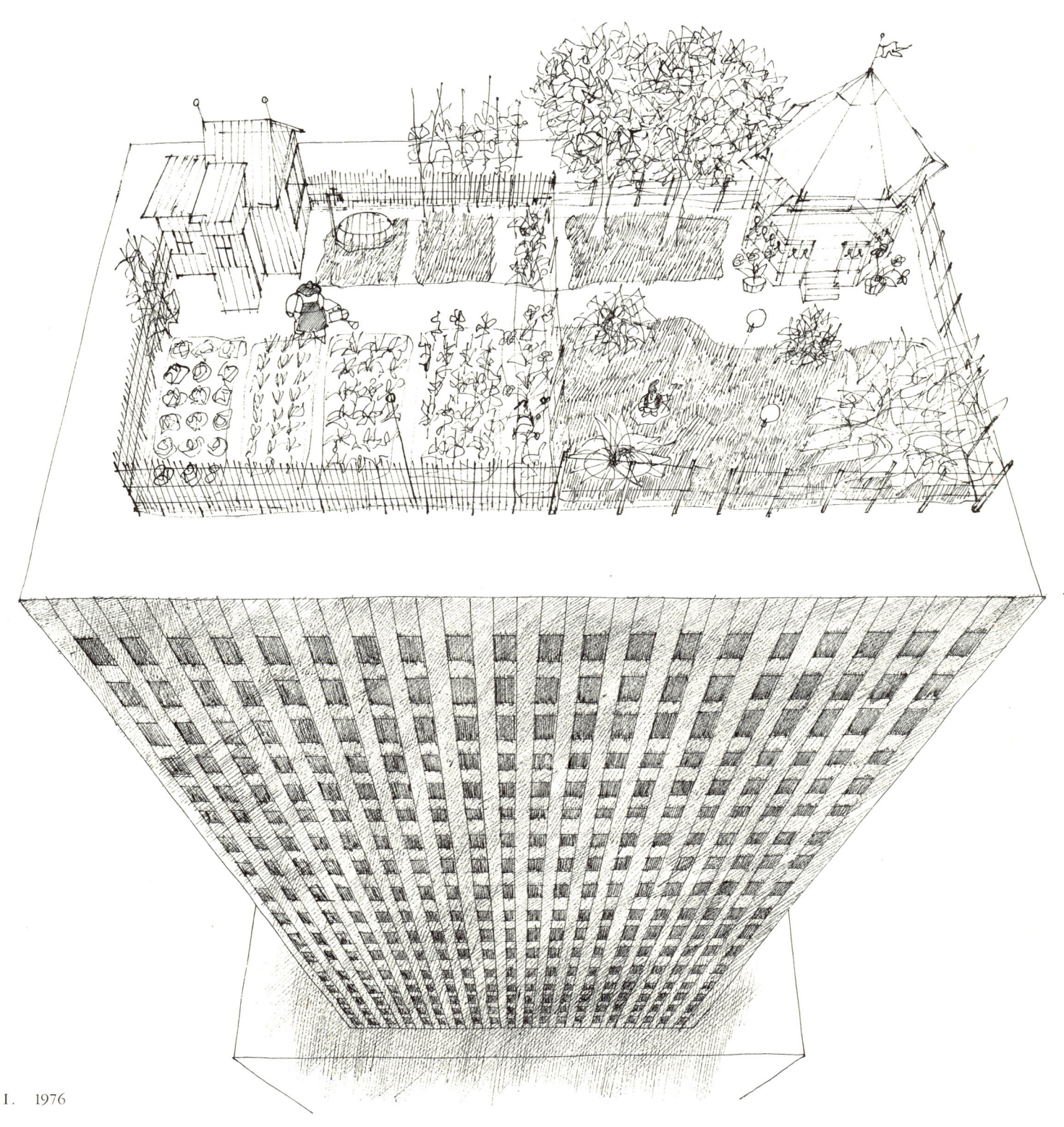

SMALLHOLDING II. 1976

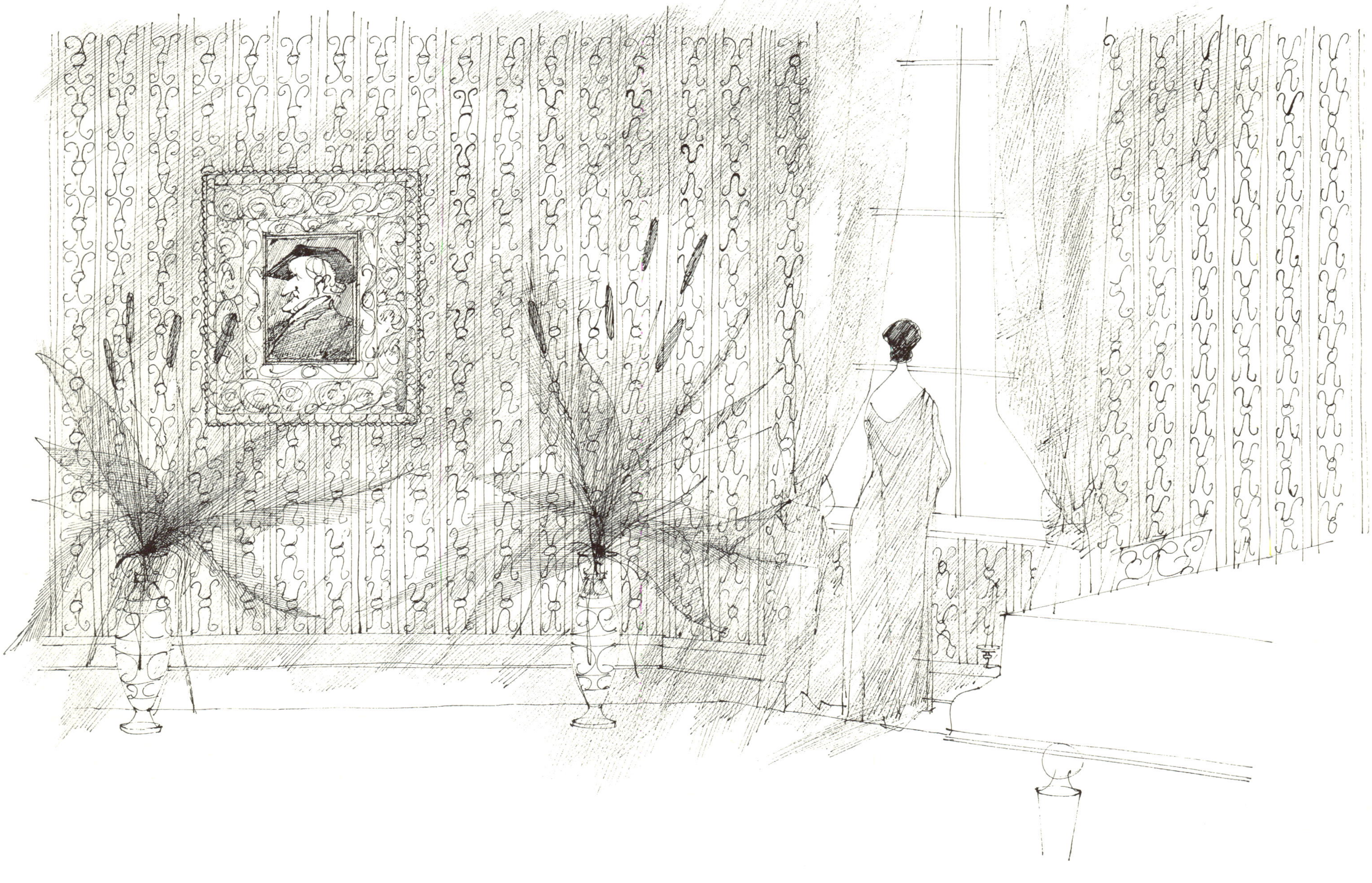

A BEAUTIFUL SOUL. 1976

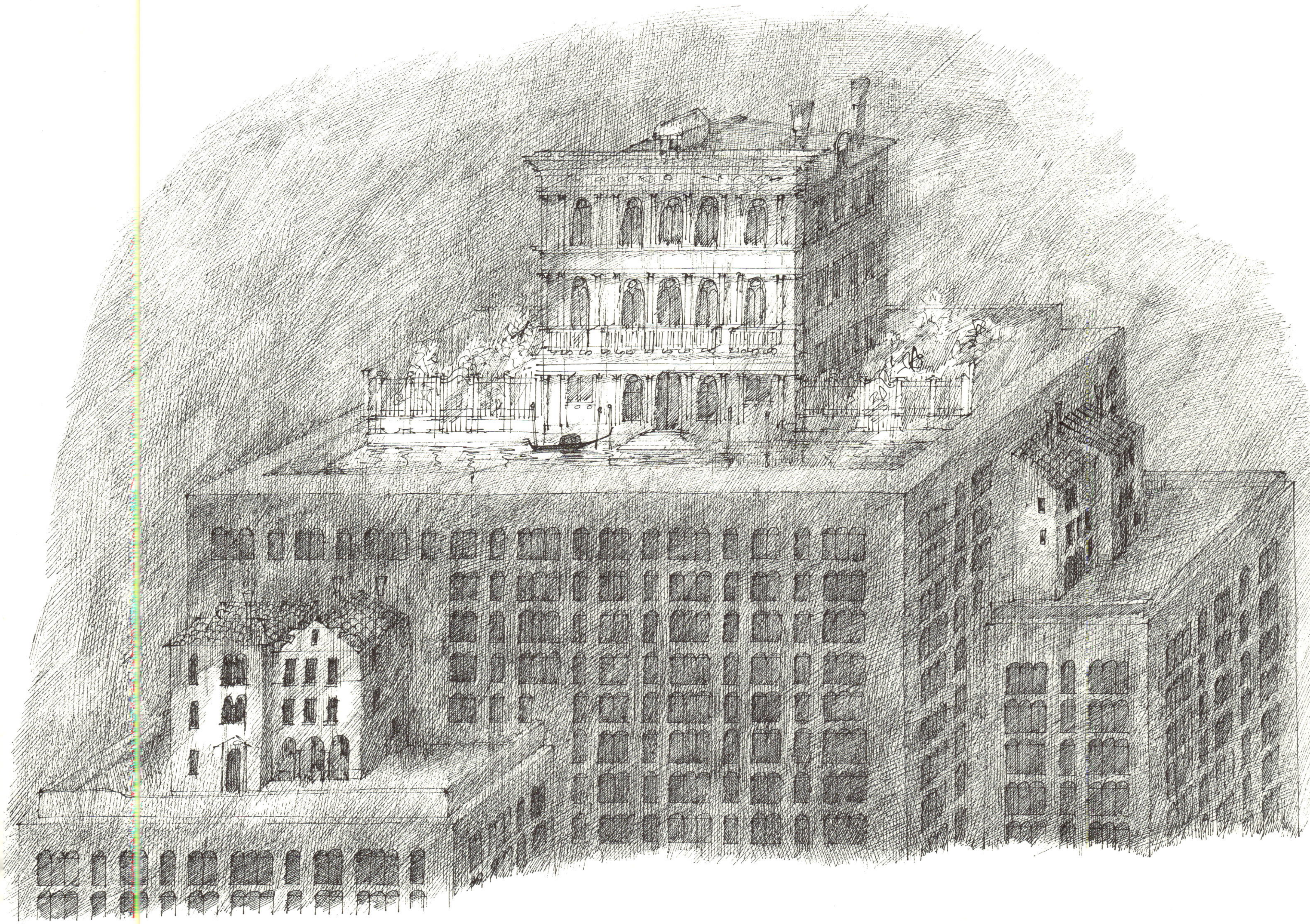

HOME FOR A WAGNERIAN. 1976

CLOUD-WREATHED MONUMENT. 1976

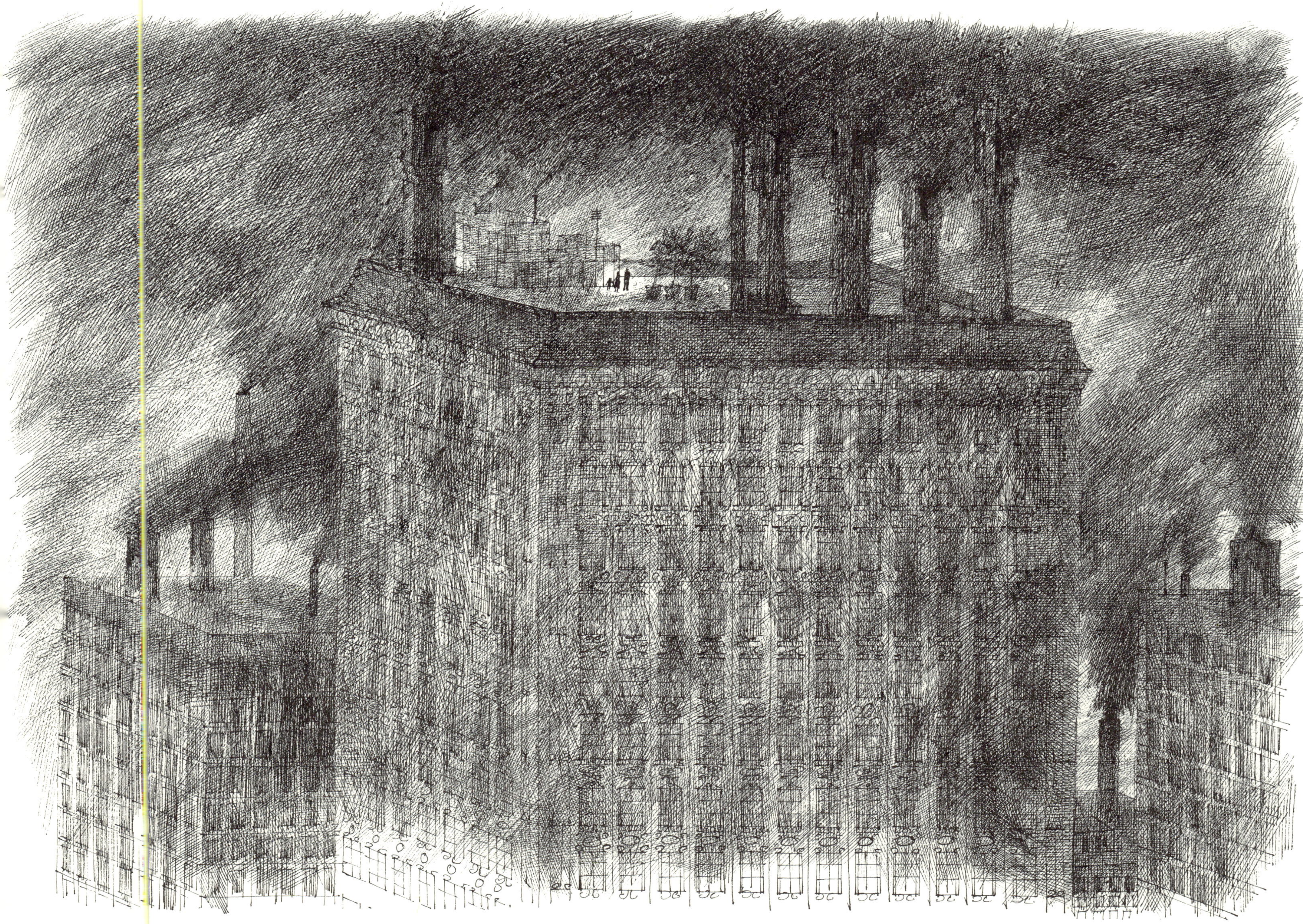

HAPPY FAMILY. 1974

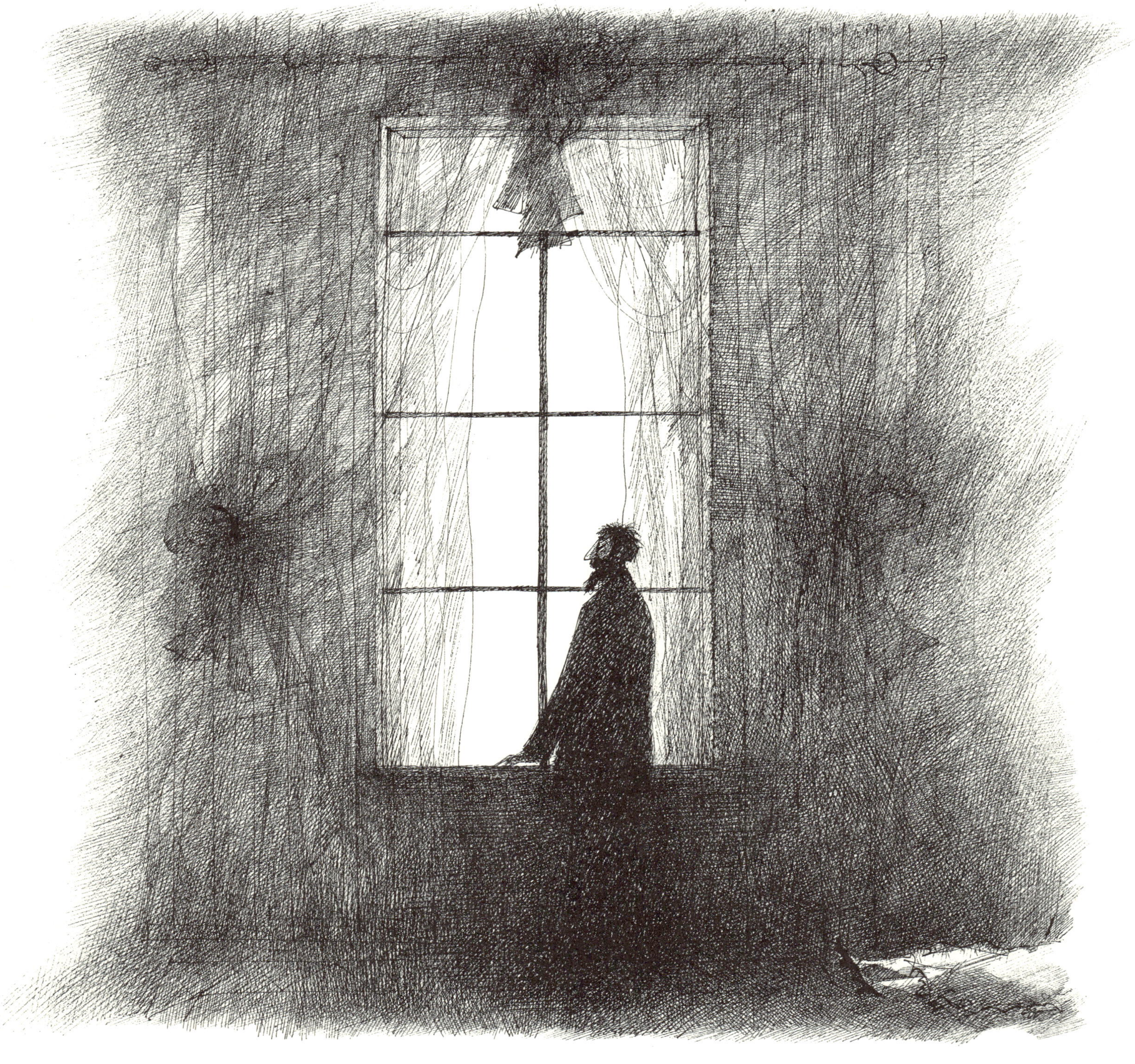

A DOMESTIC TRAGEDY. 1975

MAN AND WIFE CONTEMPLATING THE MOON. 1974

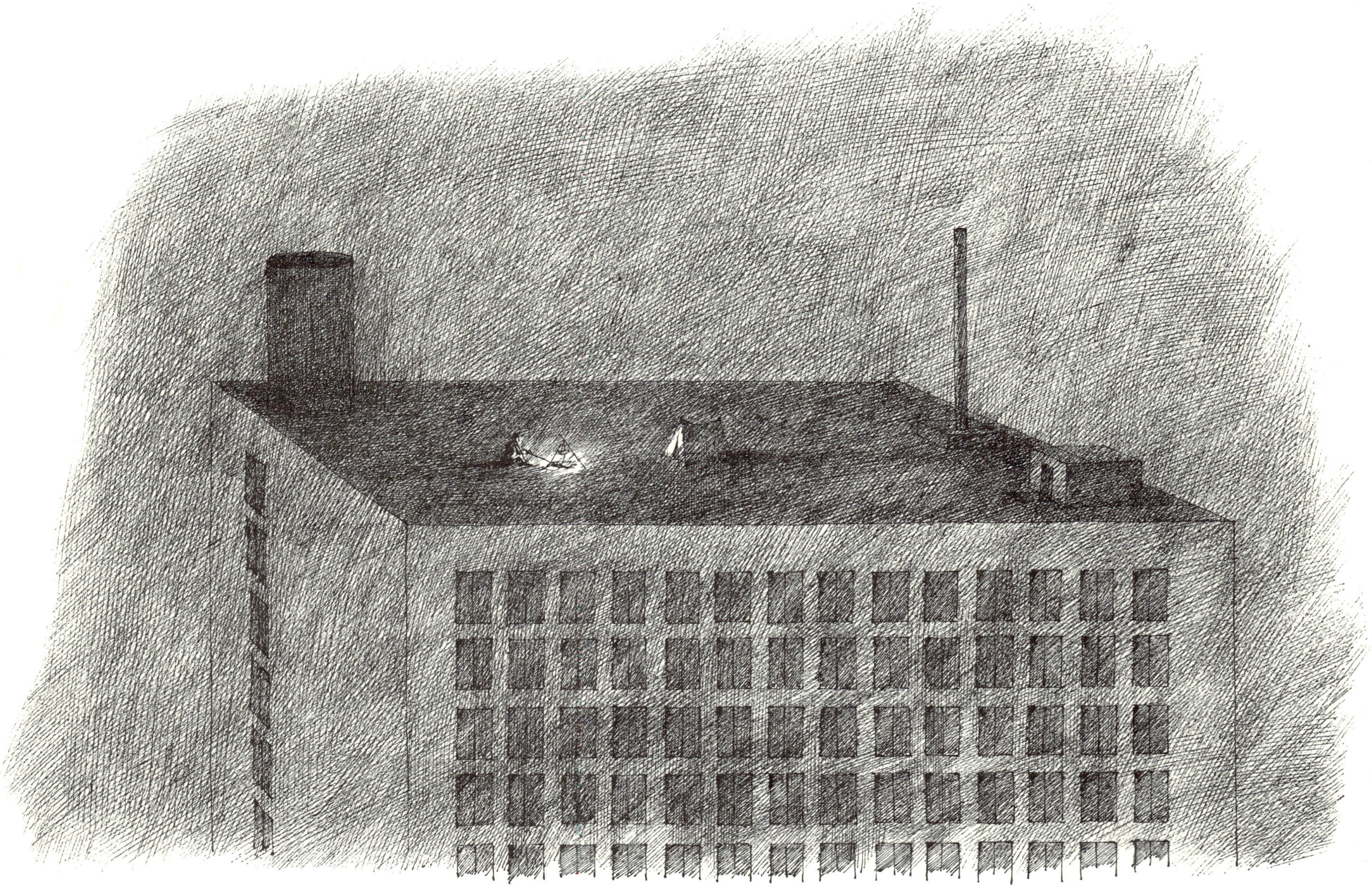

ADVENTURE. 1976

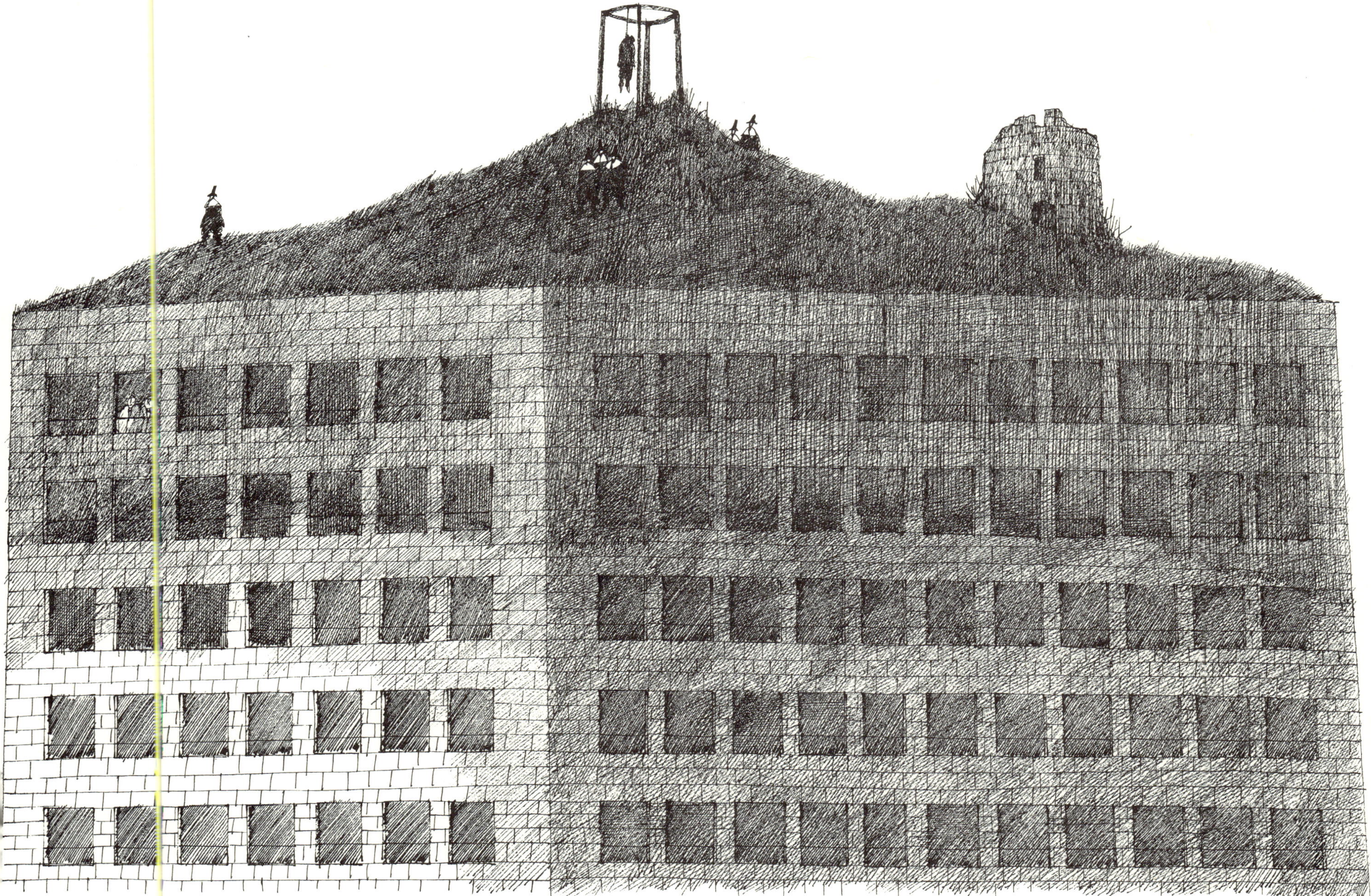

DEAR DEAD DAYS. 1976

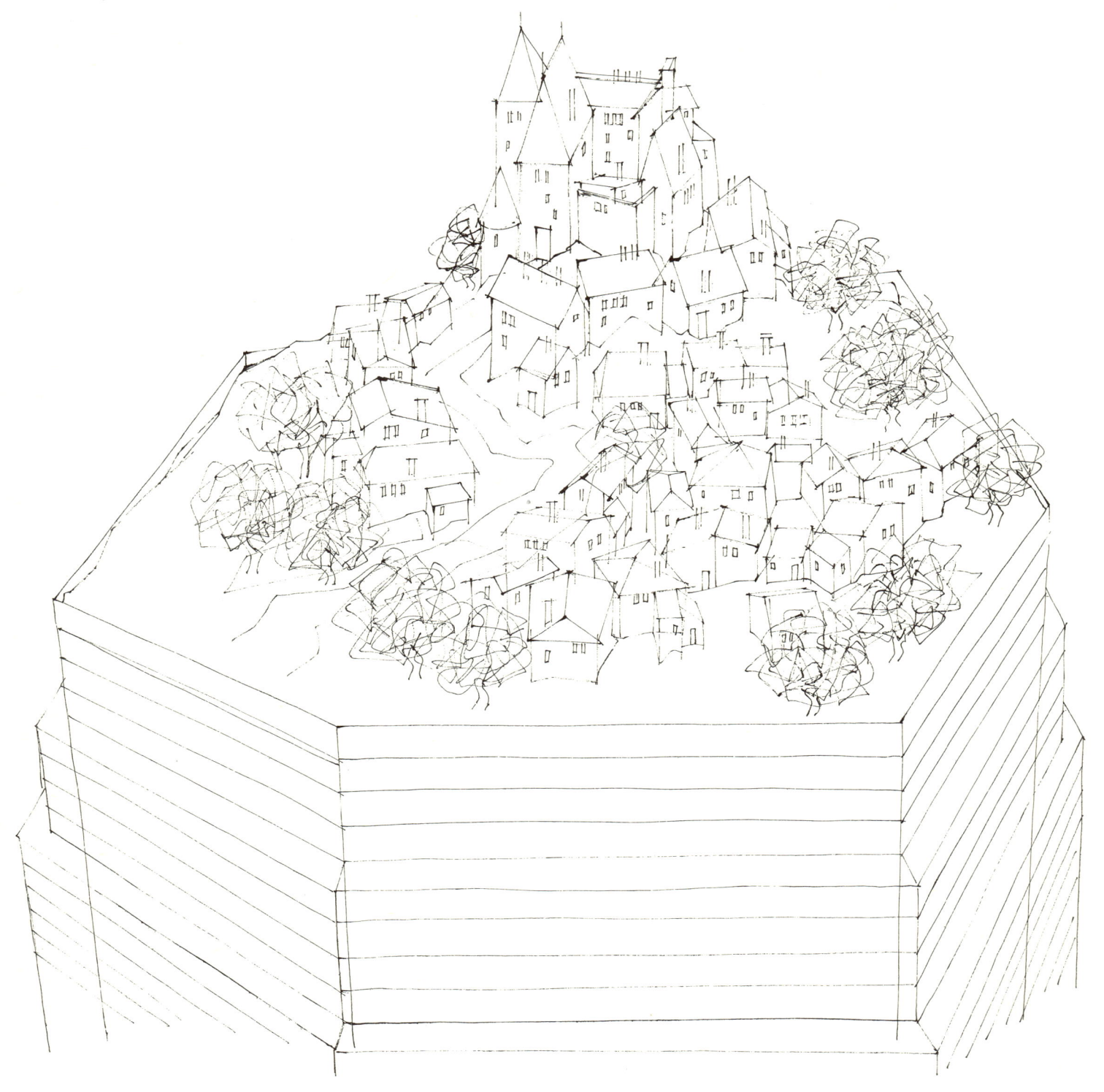

PENTVILLAGE. 1974

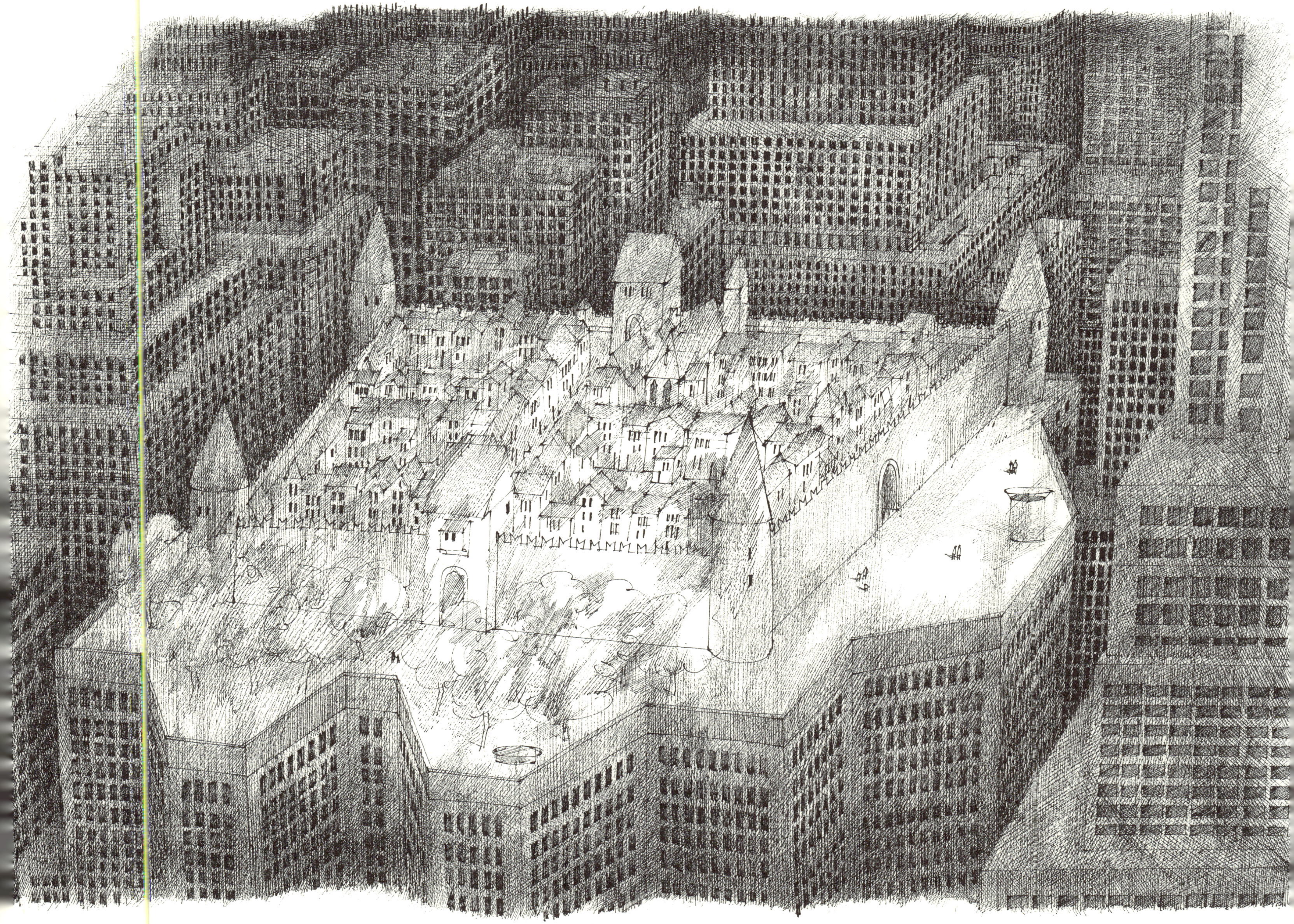

PENTTOWN. 1976

NOSTALGIC LAYOUT. 1974

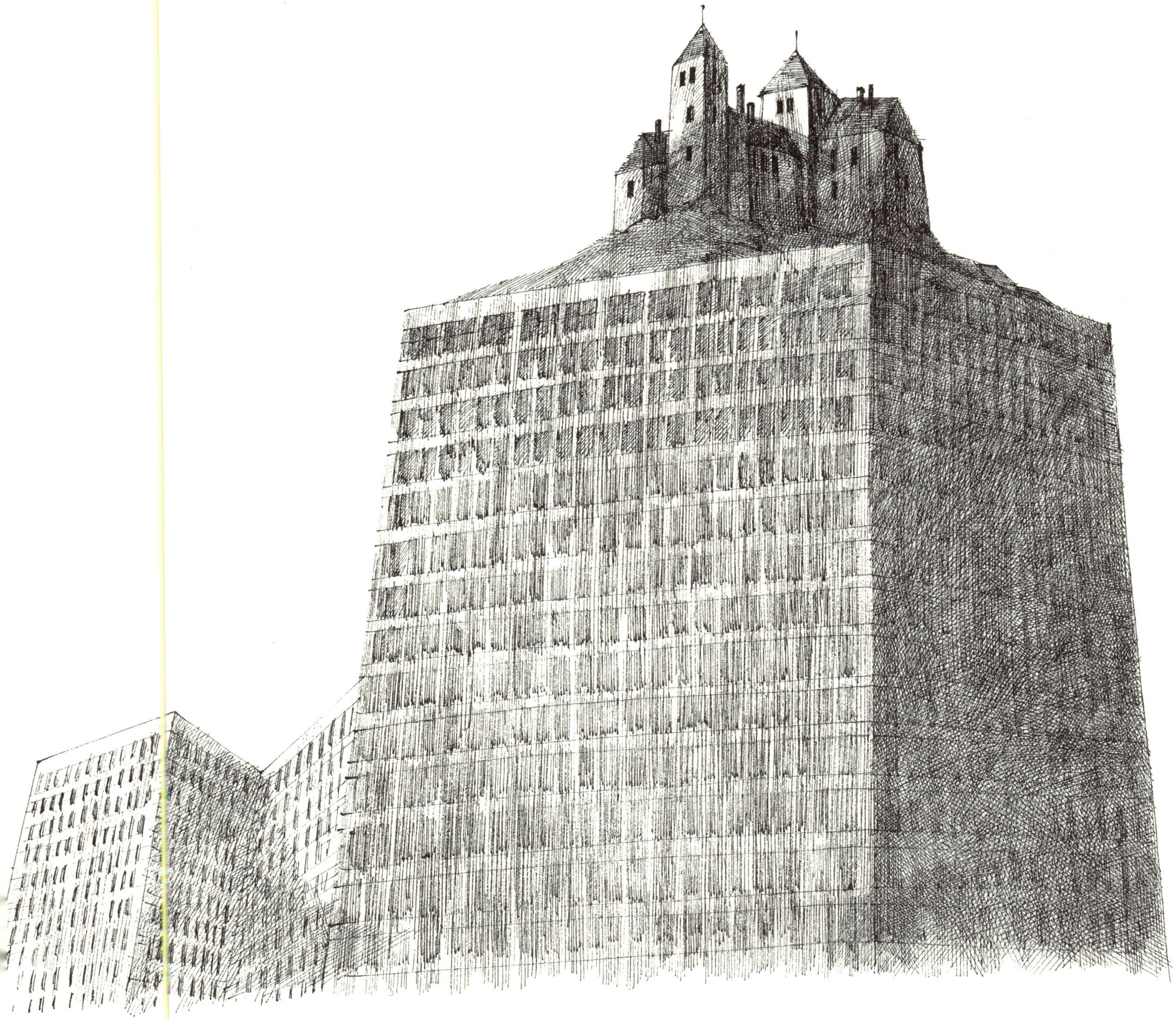

A MIGHTY FORTRESS. 1974

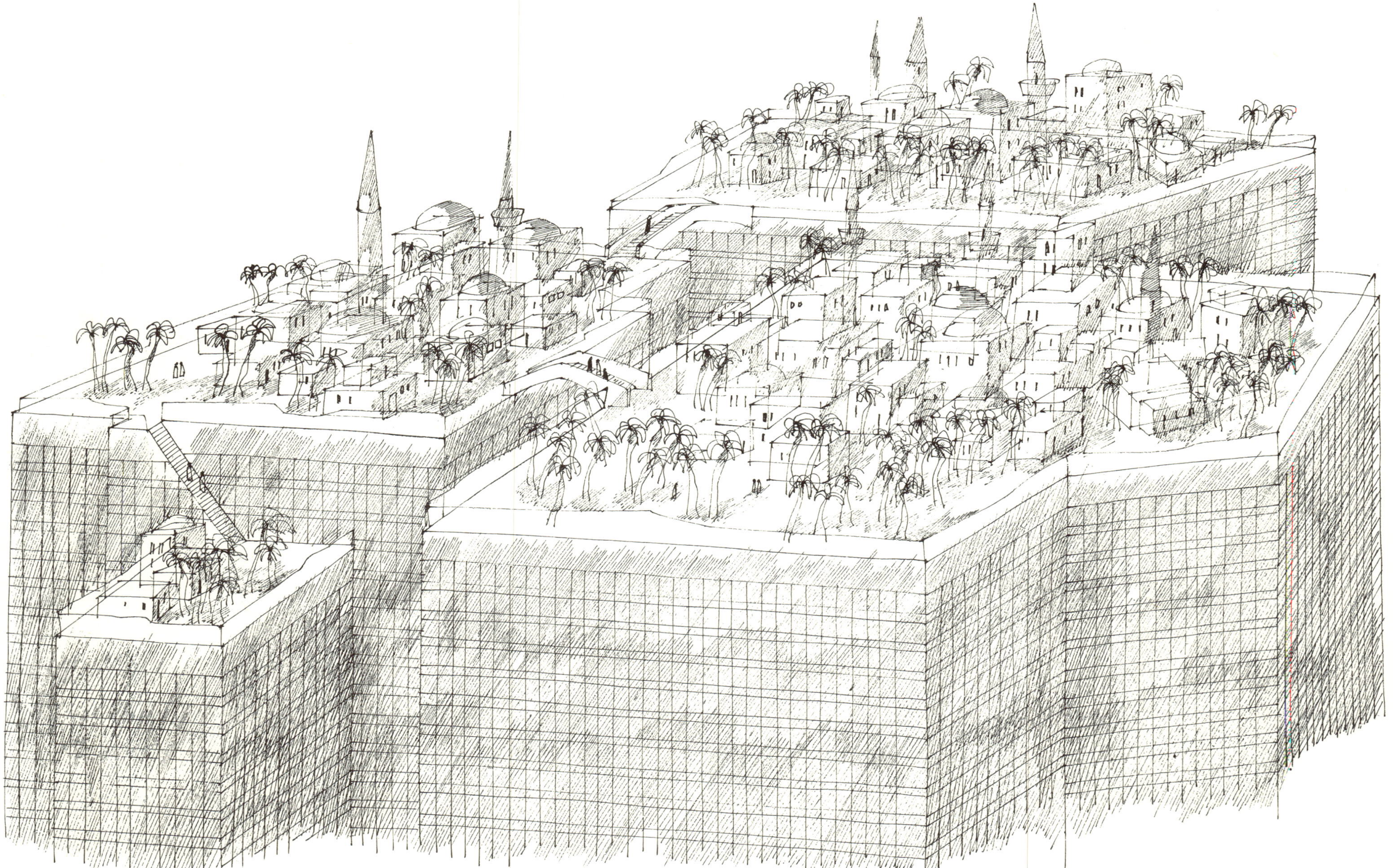

PERHAPS TIMBUKTU. 1976

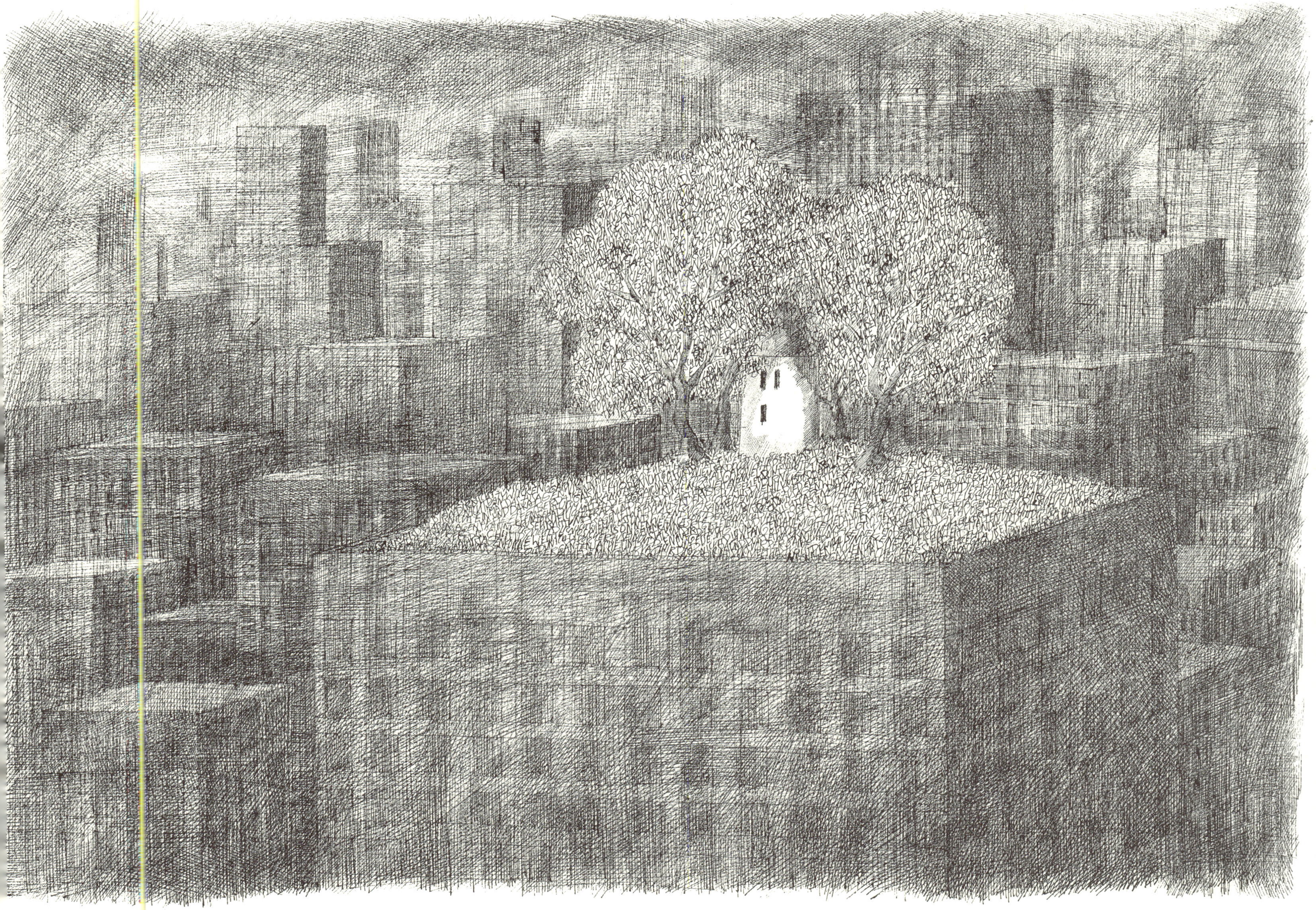

IVORY TOWER. 1974

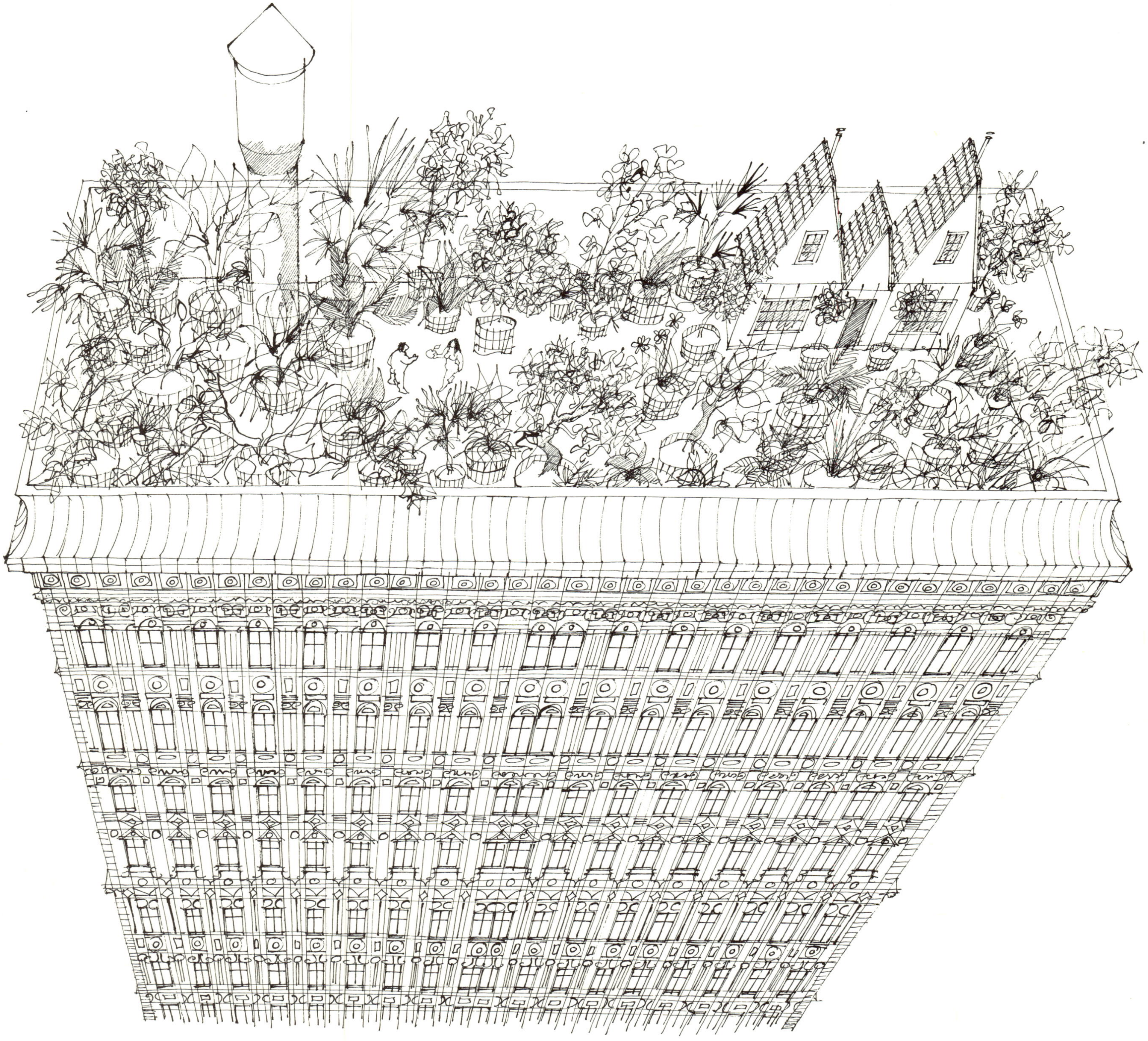

A LITTLE PARADISE. 1977

ALONE AT LAST. 1976

VAMPIRE. 1975

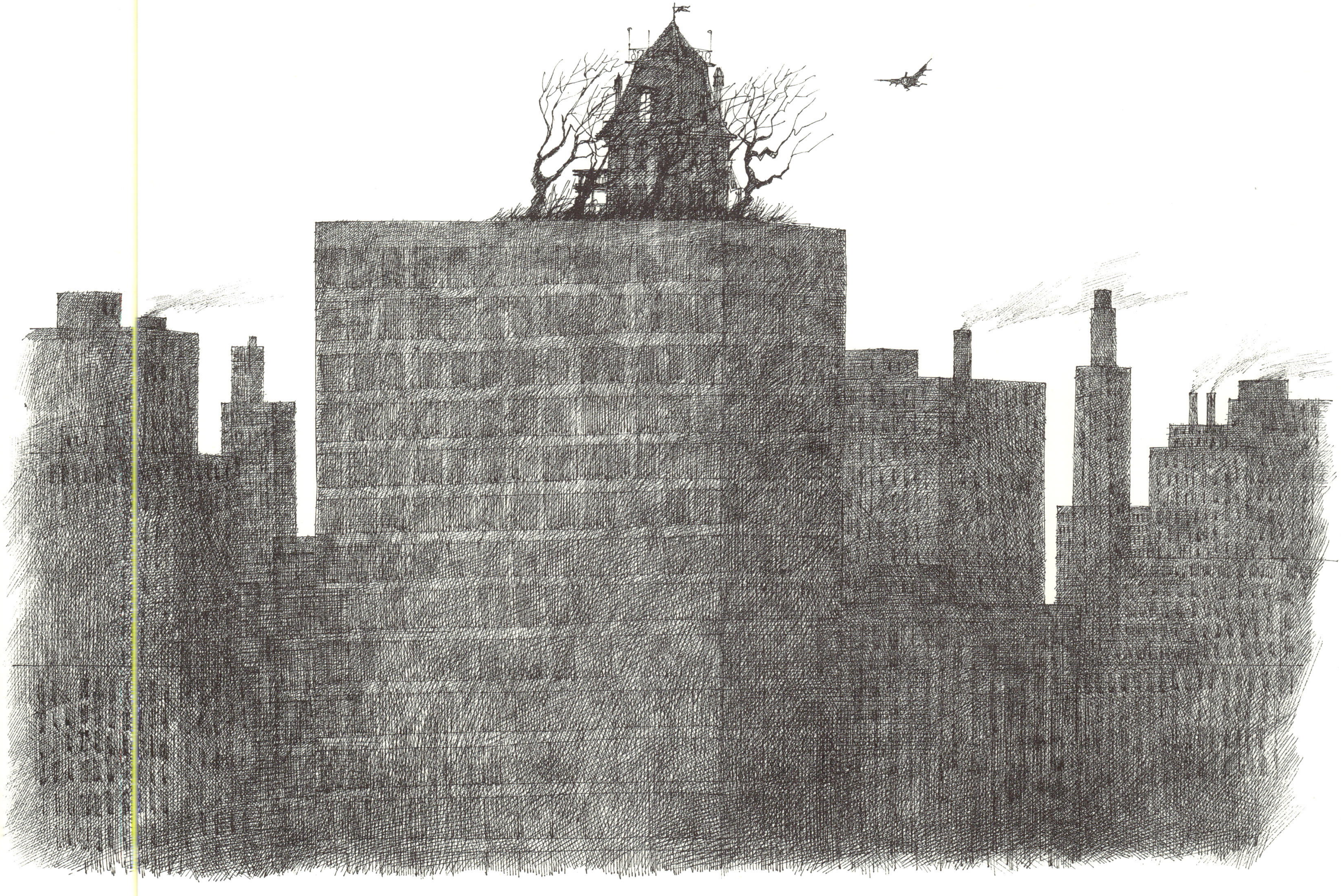

DRACULA'S HOME. 1974

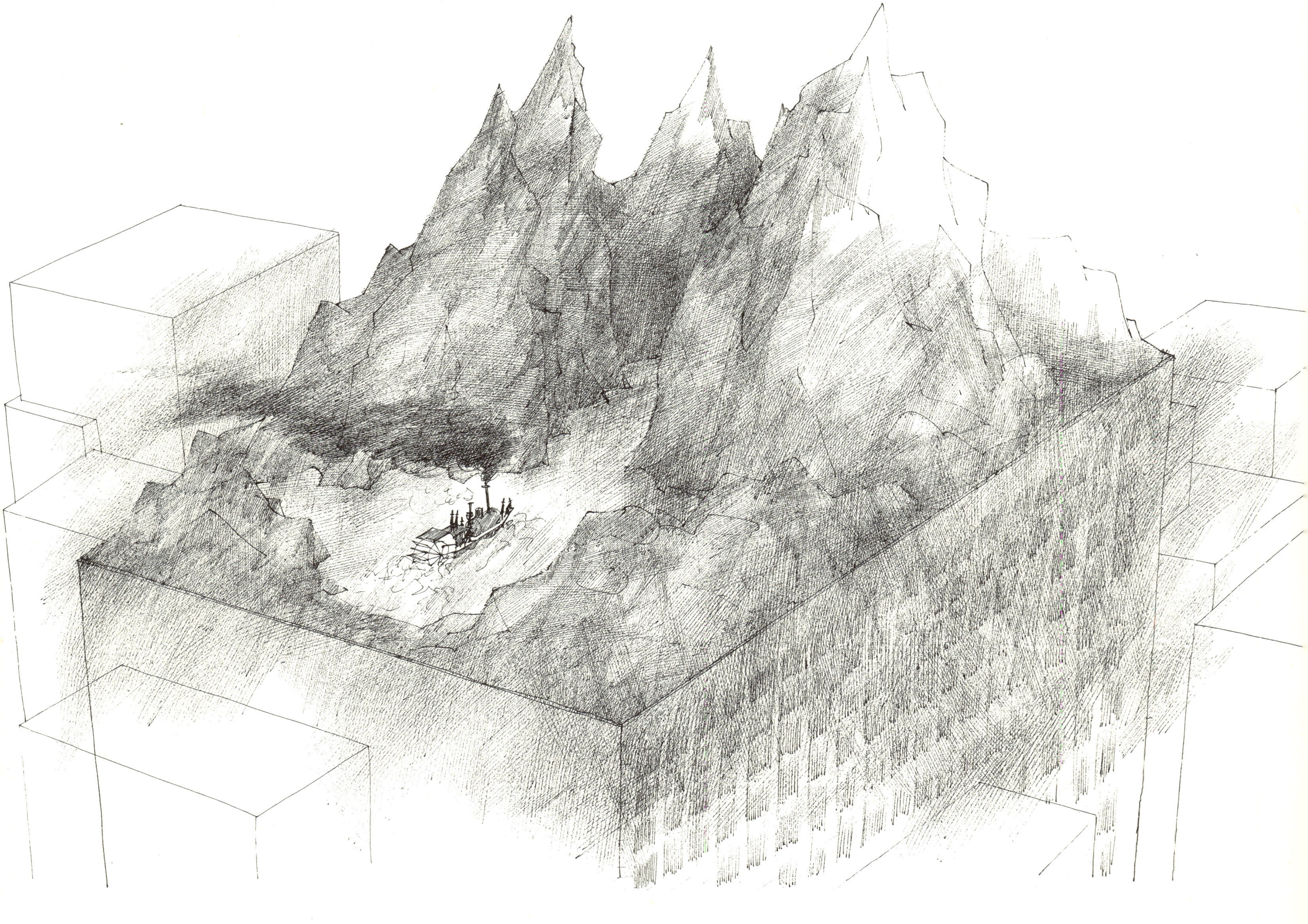

THE ADVENTURERS. 1976

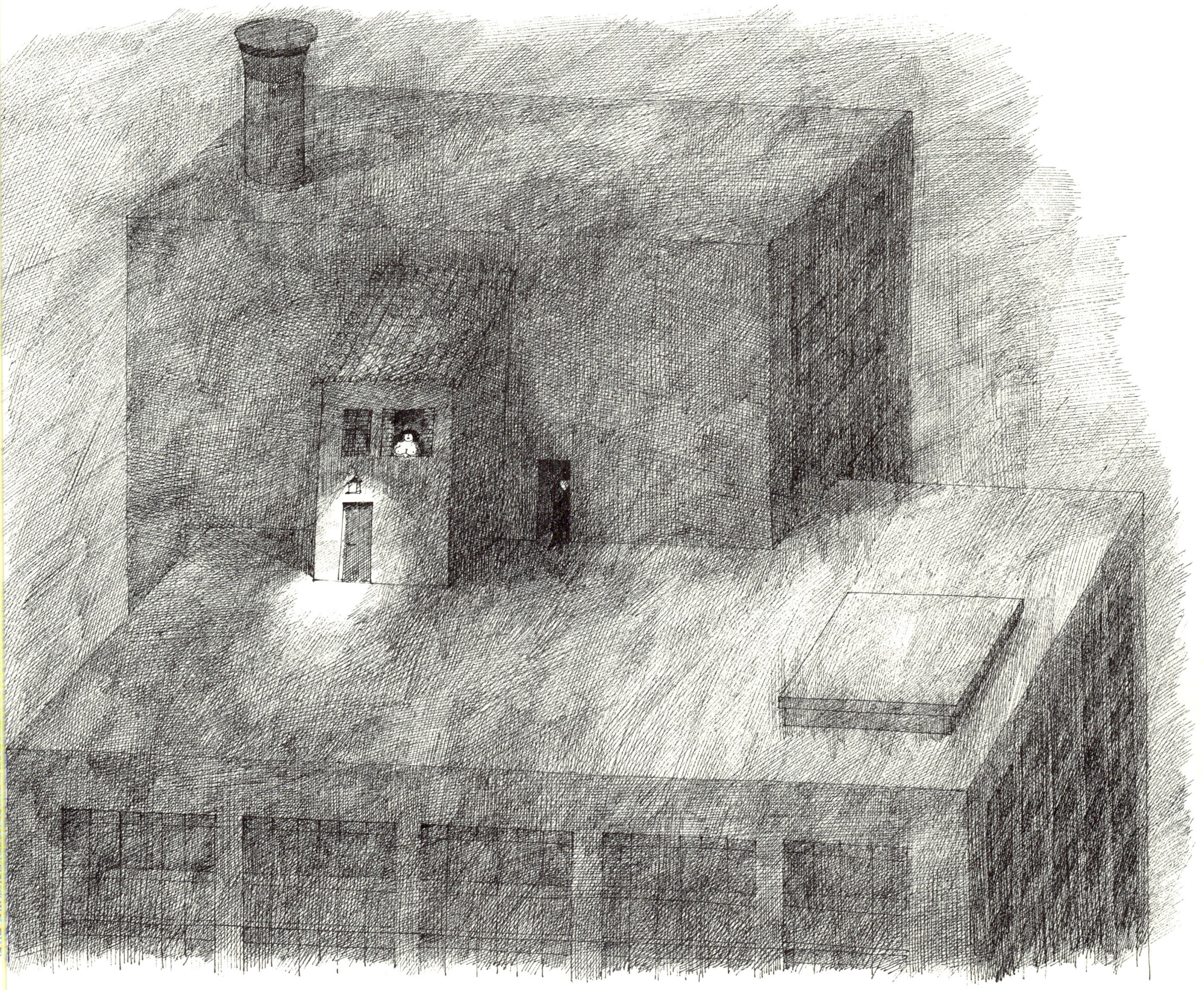

THE SUITOR. 1976

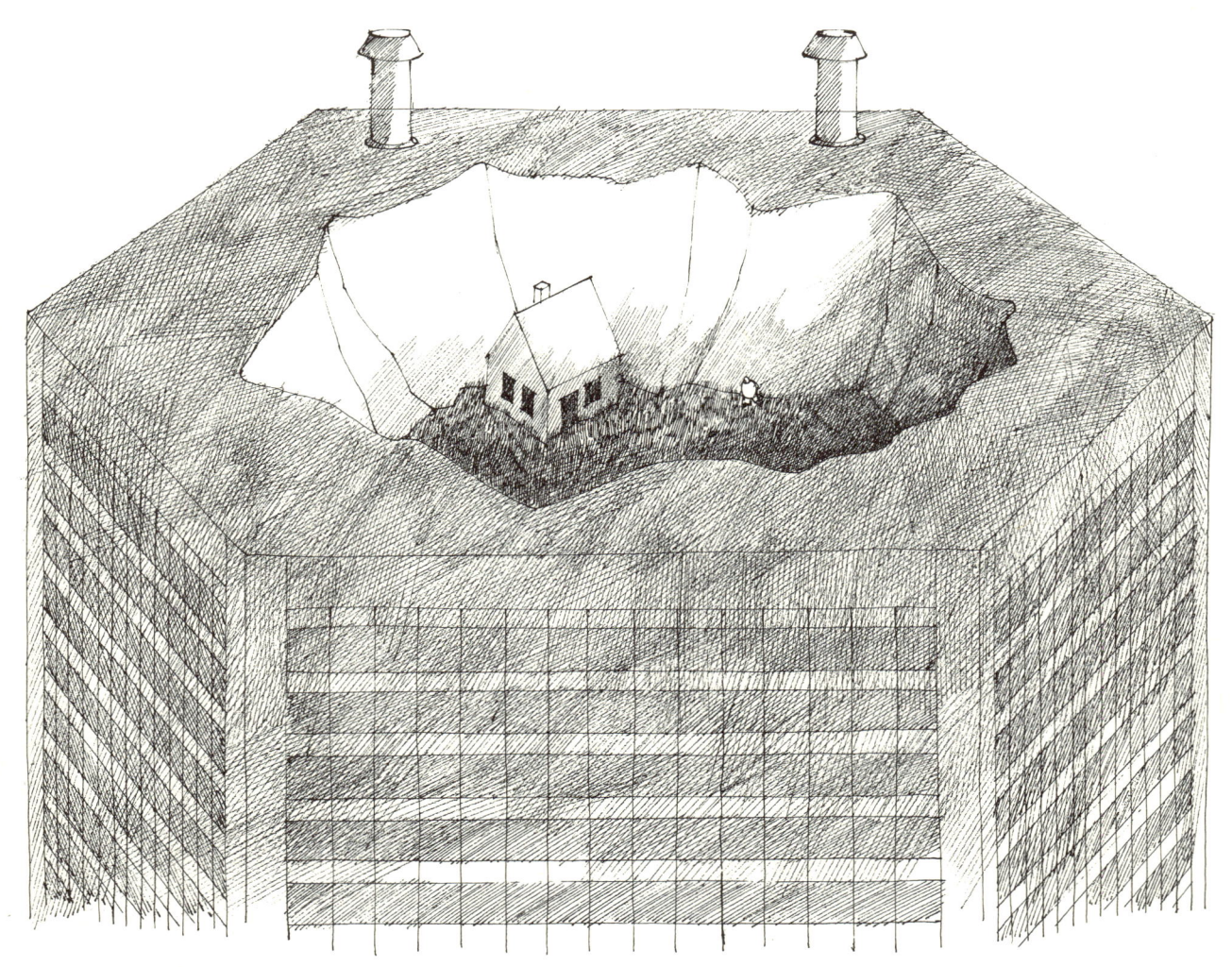

PLAN FOR AN INTROVERT. 1976

THE MOWER ON THE MOUNTAIN. 1976

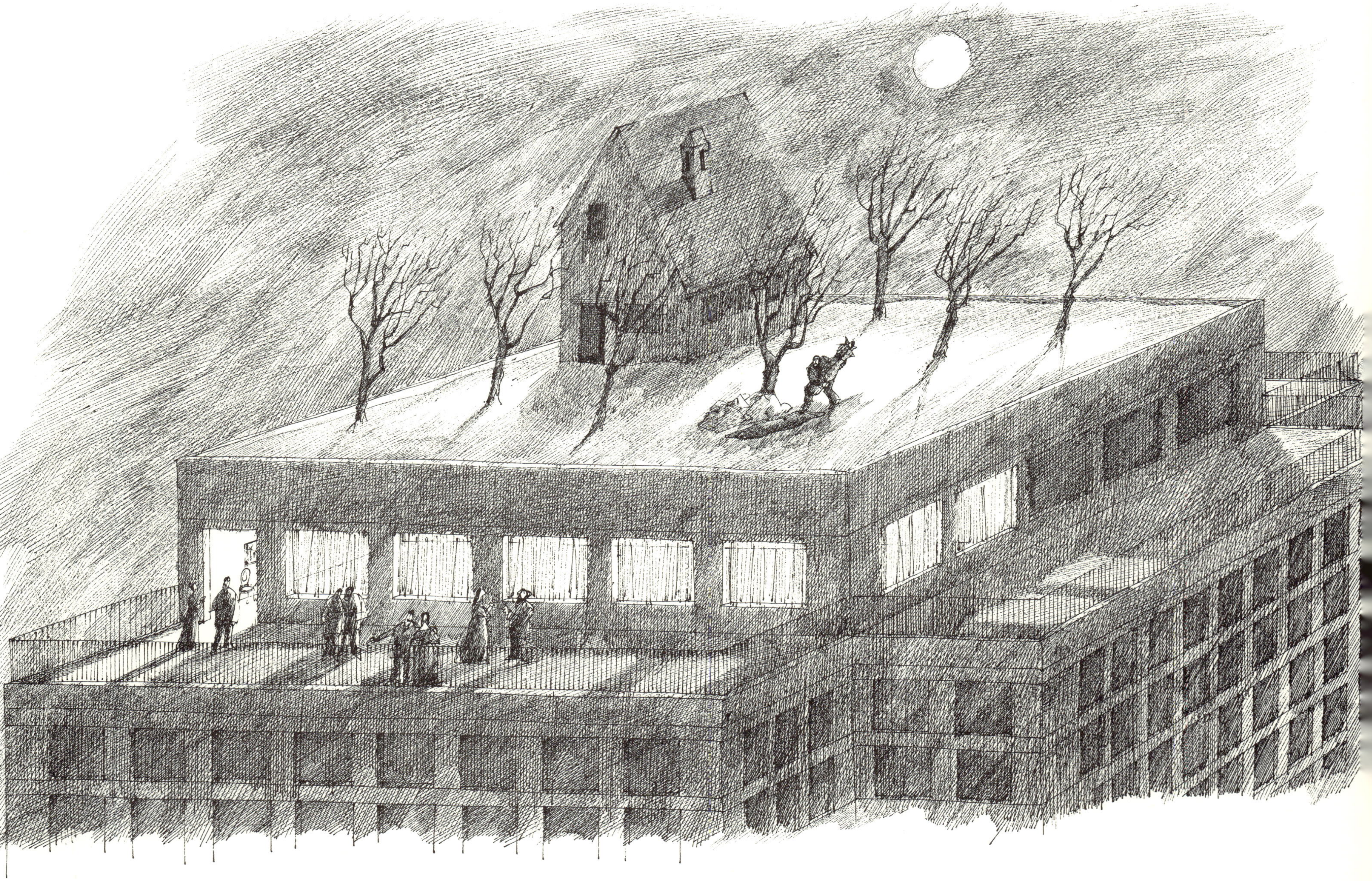

UNDER THE PEAR TREE. 1976

BEFORE THE CATASTROPHE. 1976

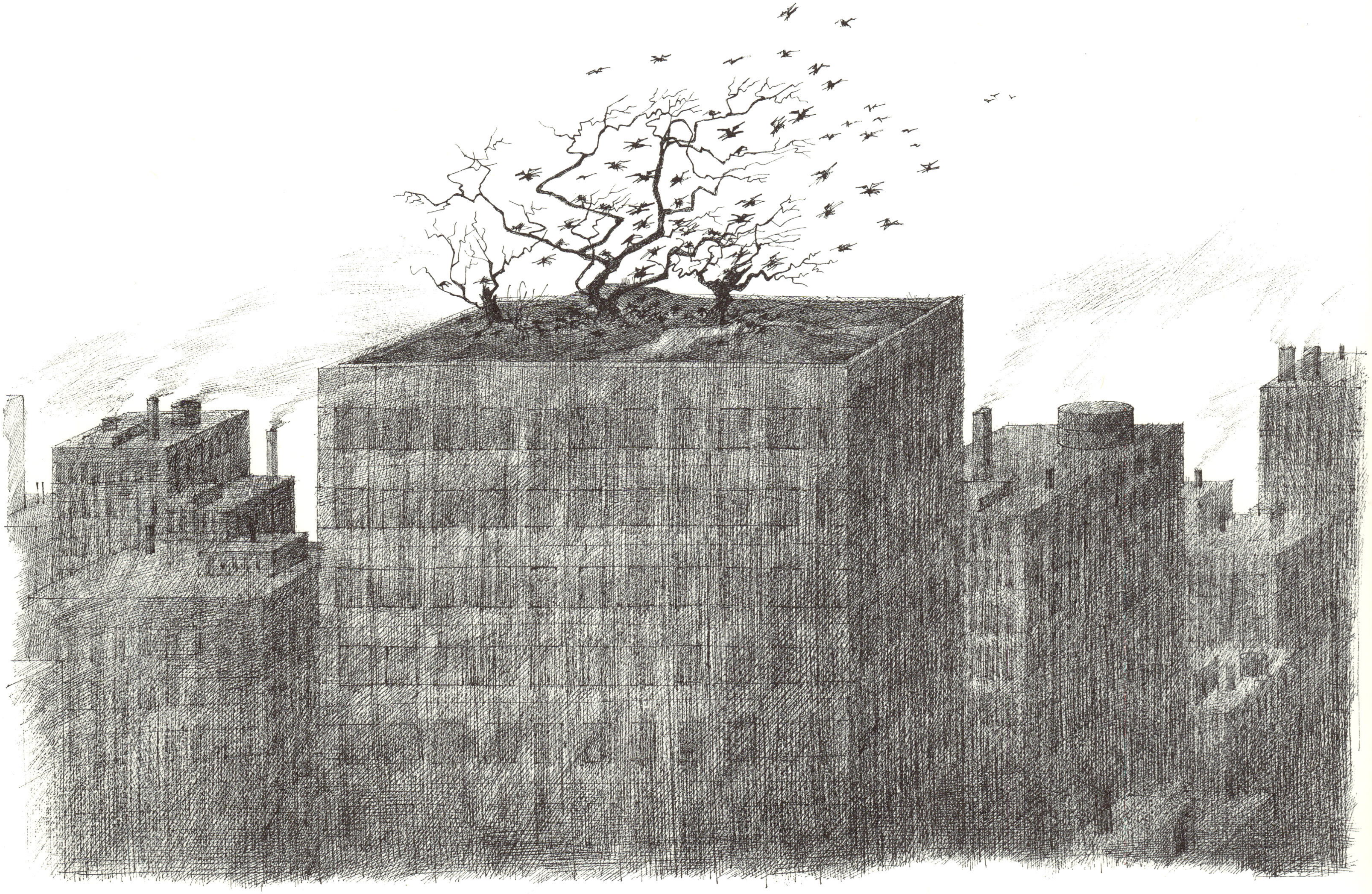

HEATH ROAD. 1974

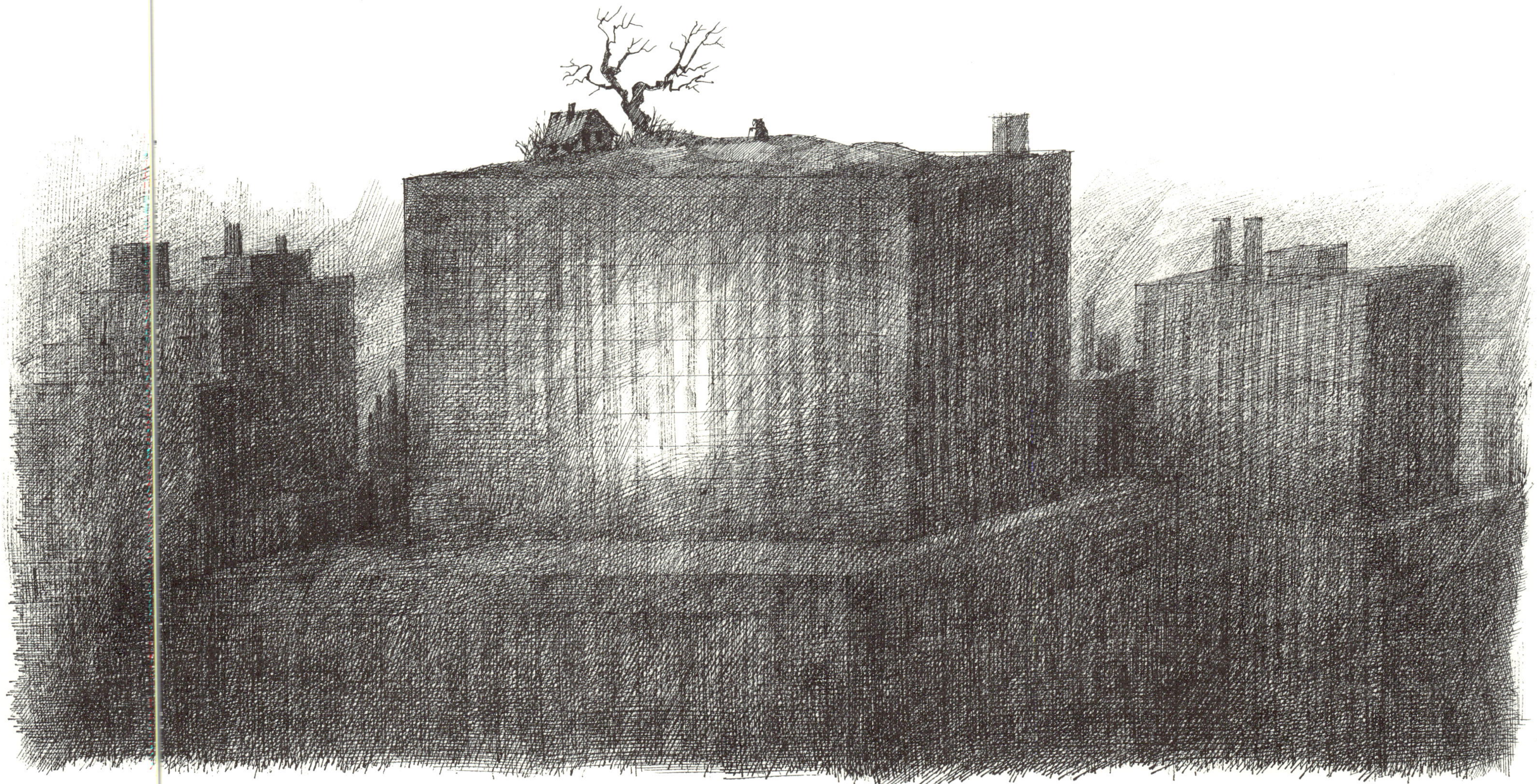

WITCH'S HOUSE. 1974

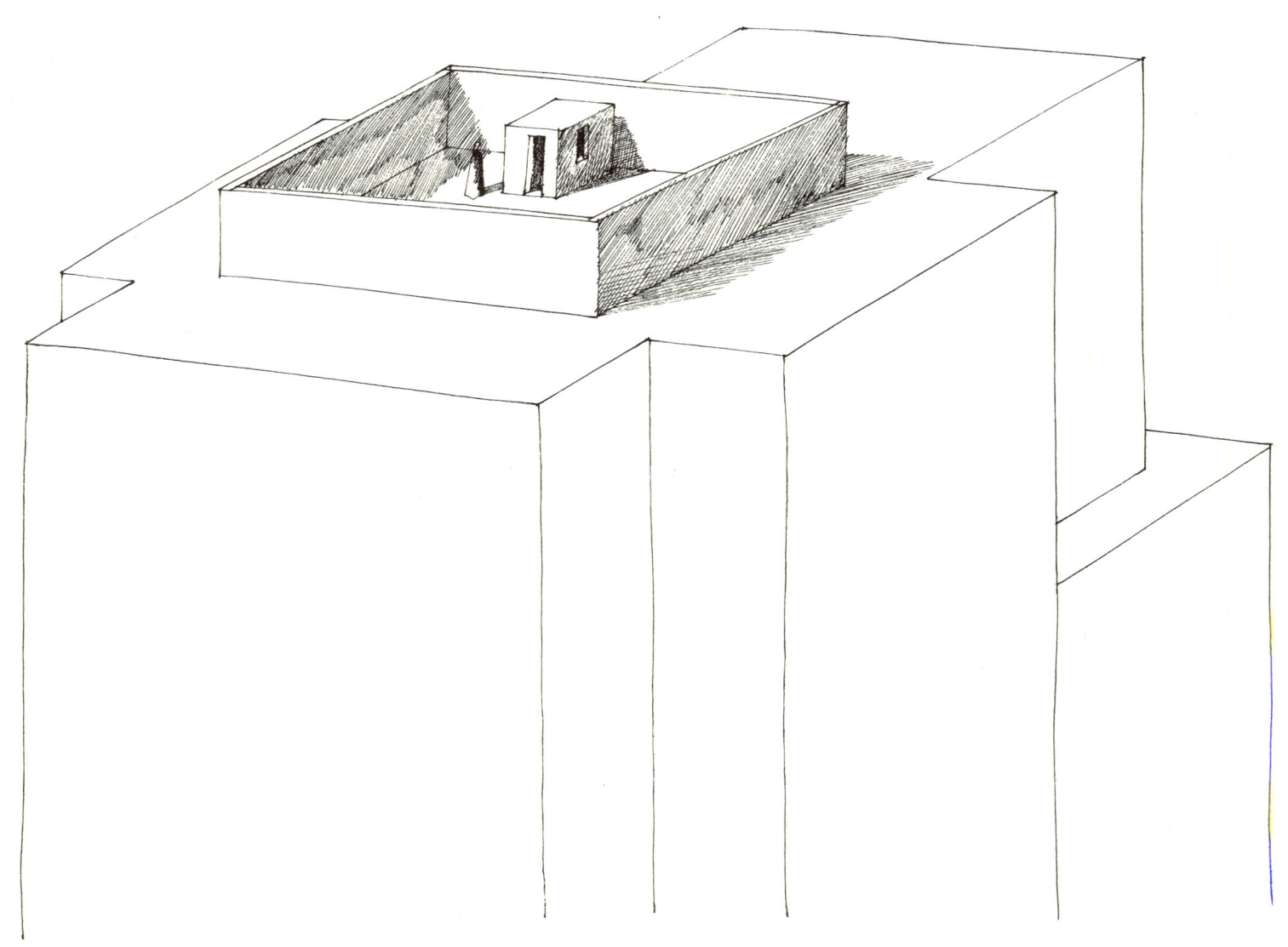

LAYOUT FOR A HERMIT. 1976

AN AGGLOMERATION OF HERMITS. 1976

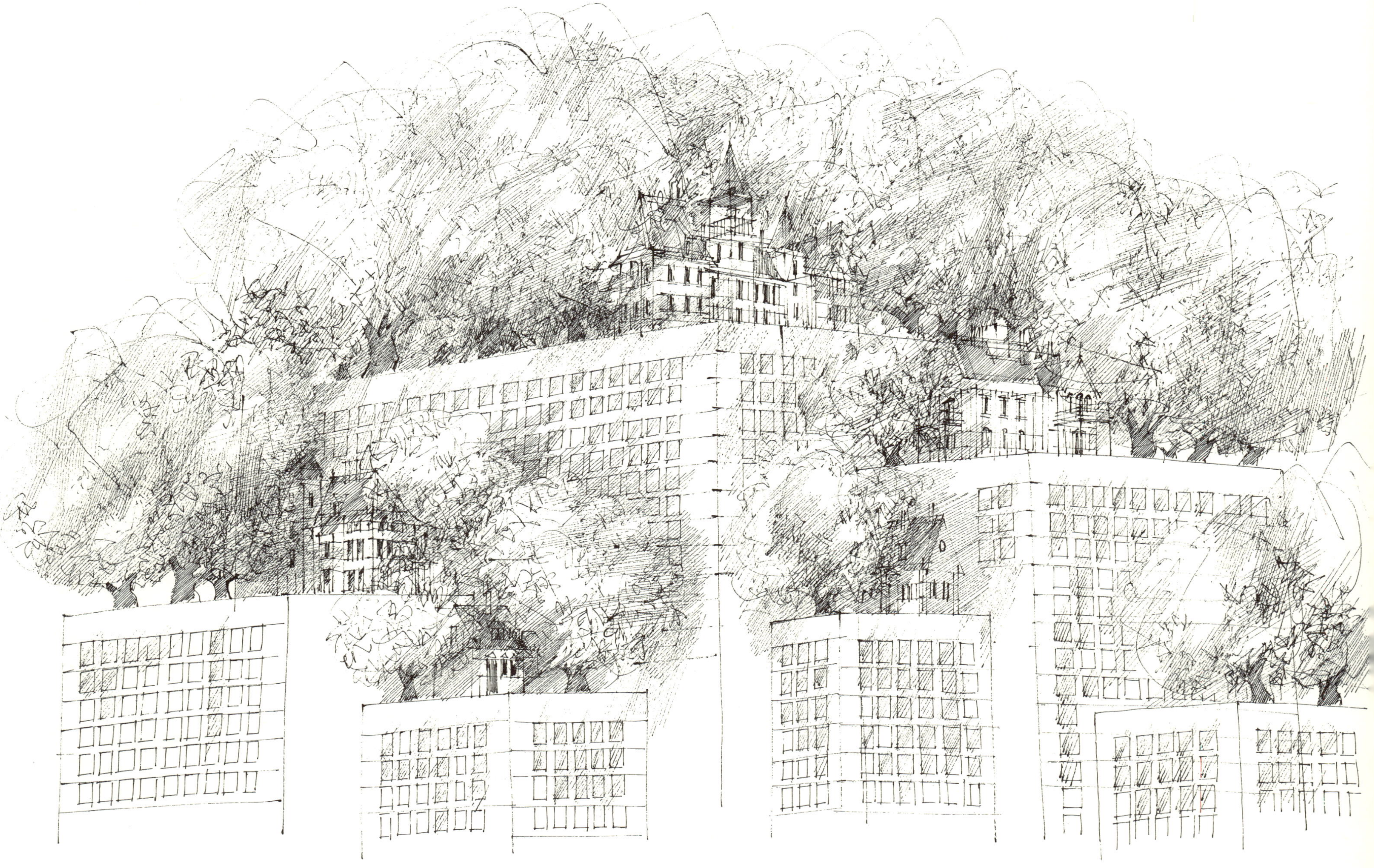

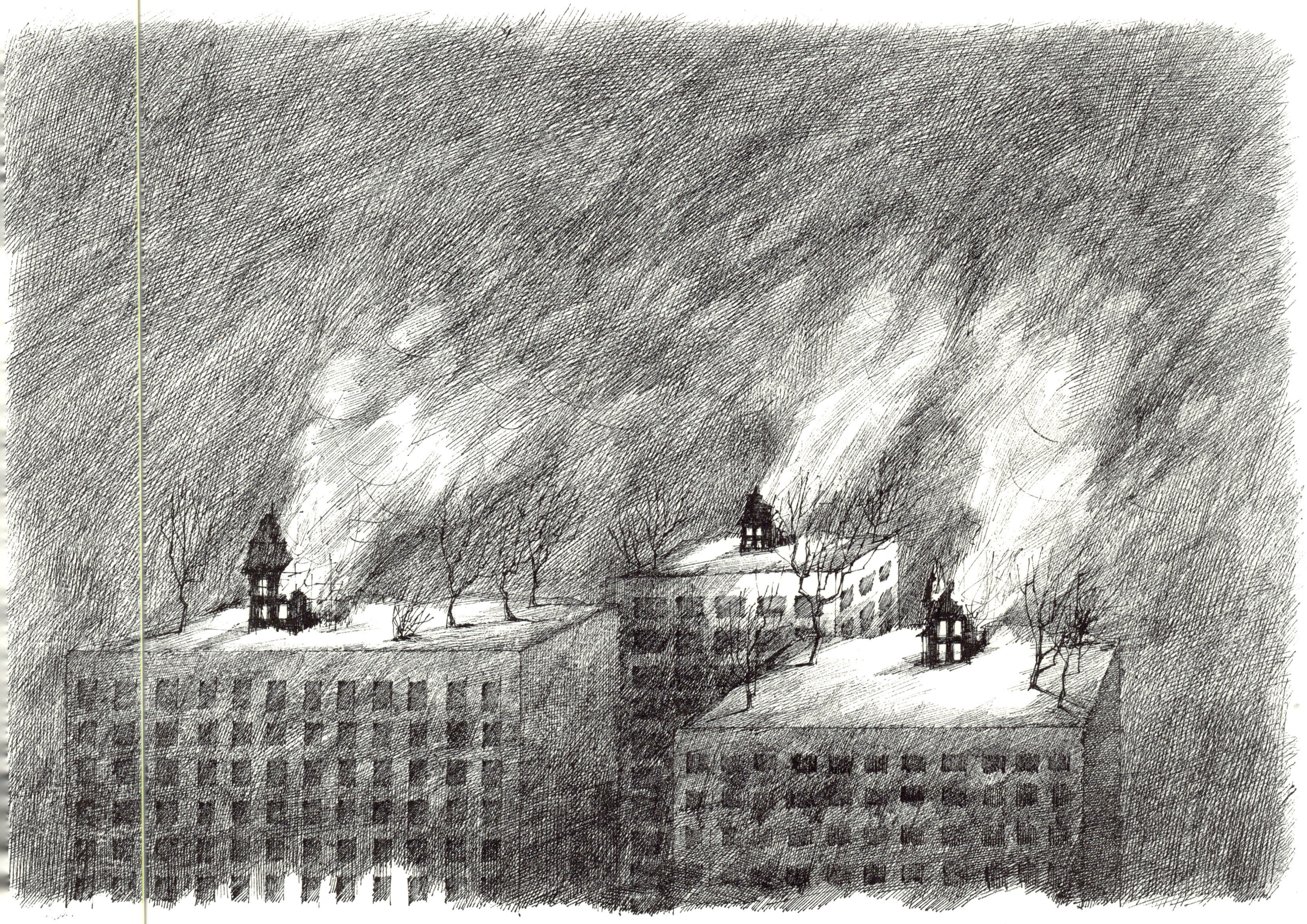

CONFLAGRATION. 1974

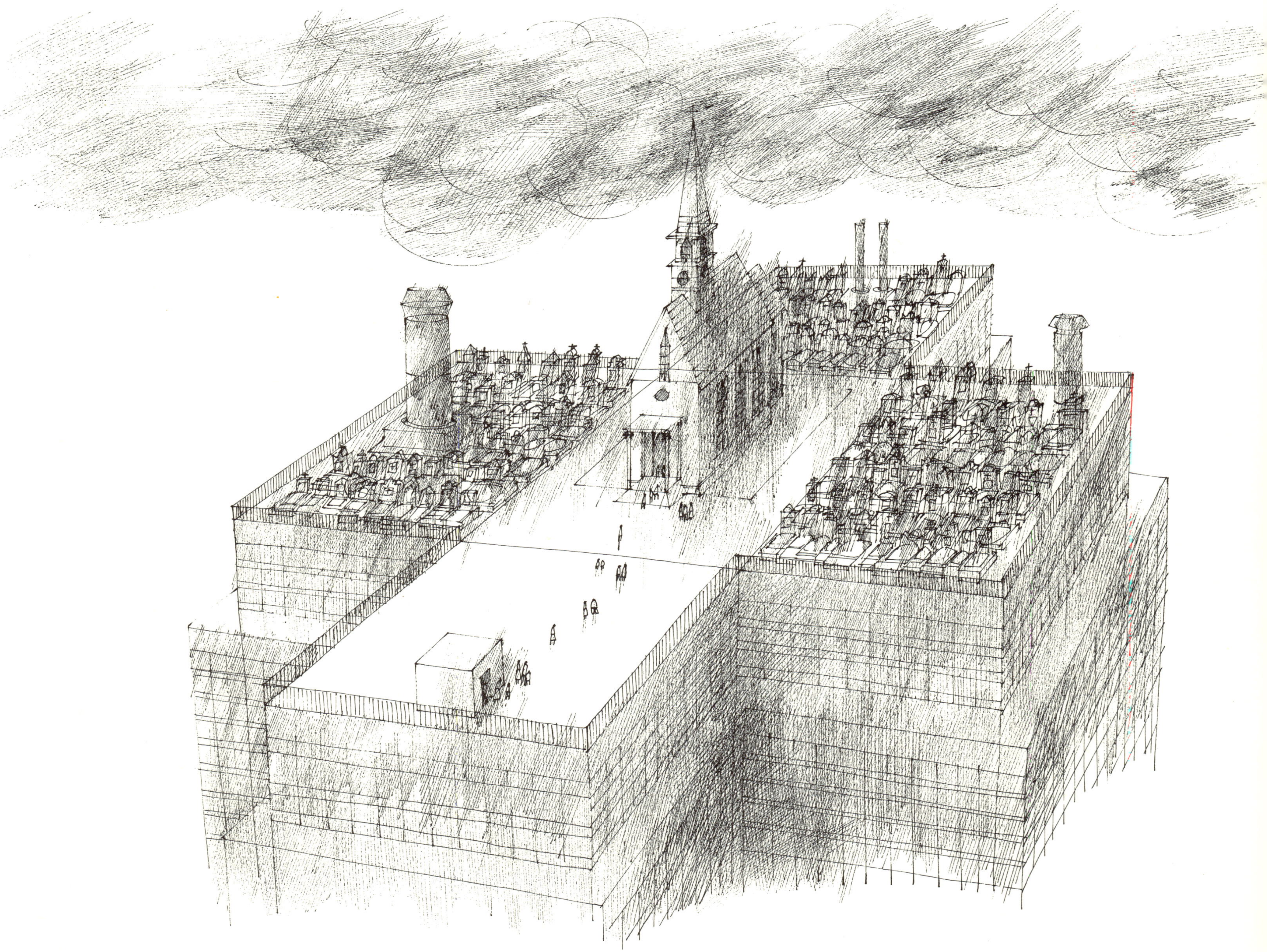

CHURCHGOING. 1976

WIDOW. 1970

SCARING RAVENS IN WINTER. 1976

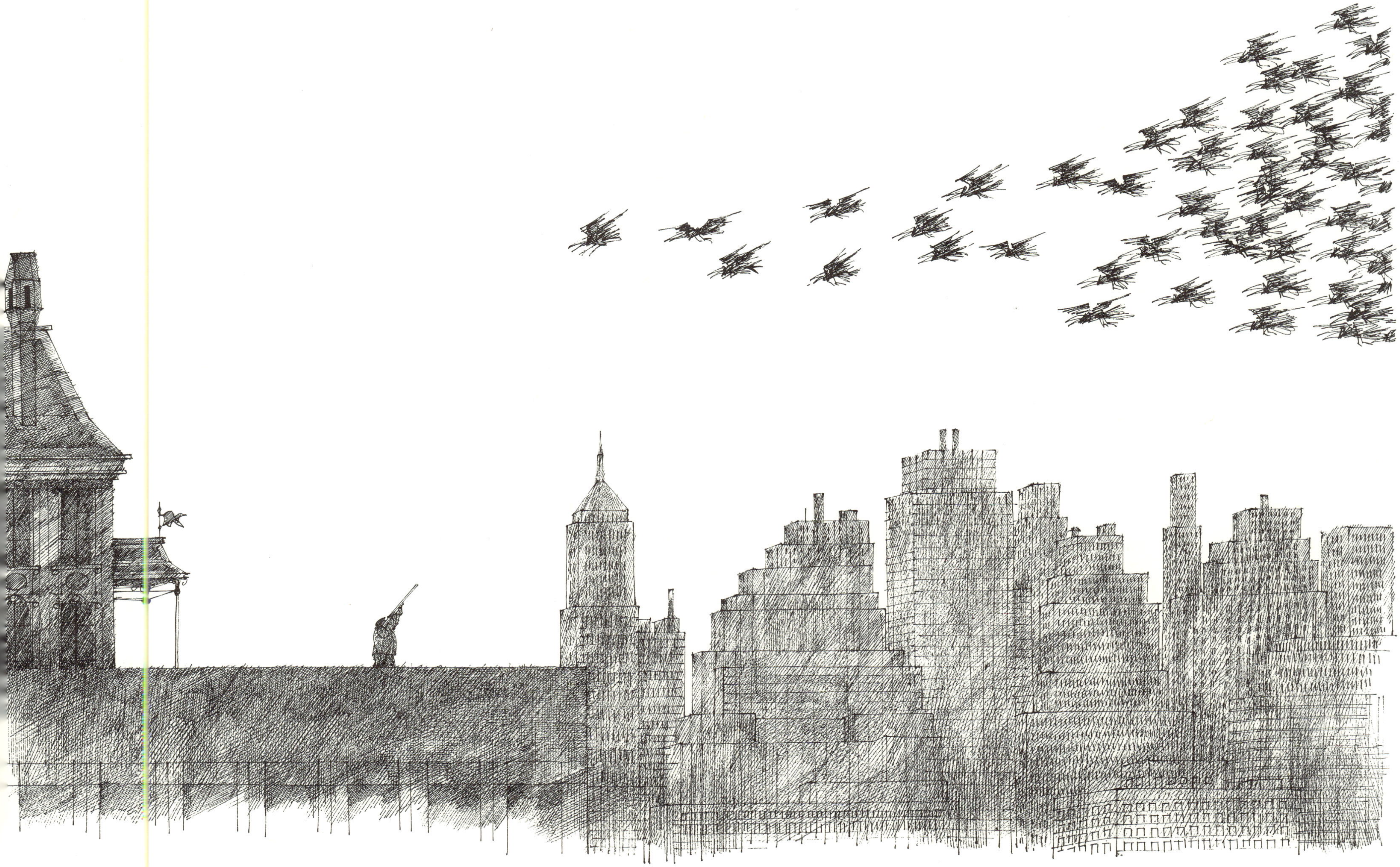

RAVEN HUNTER. 1976

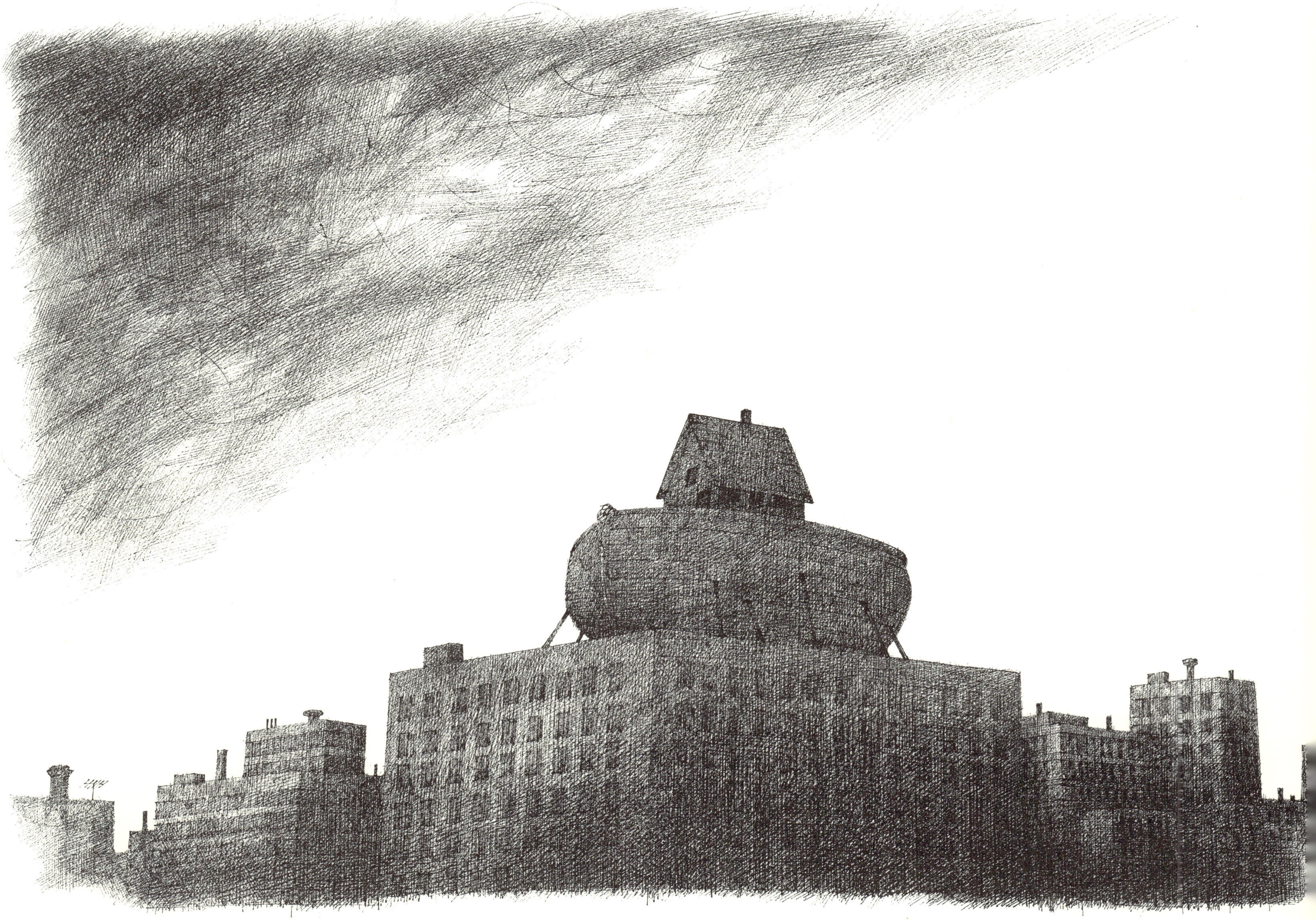

EXPECTATION. 1974

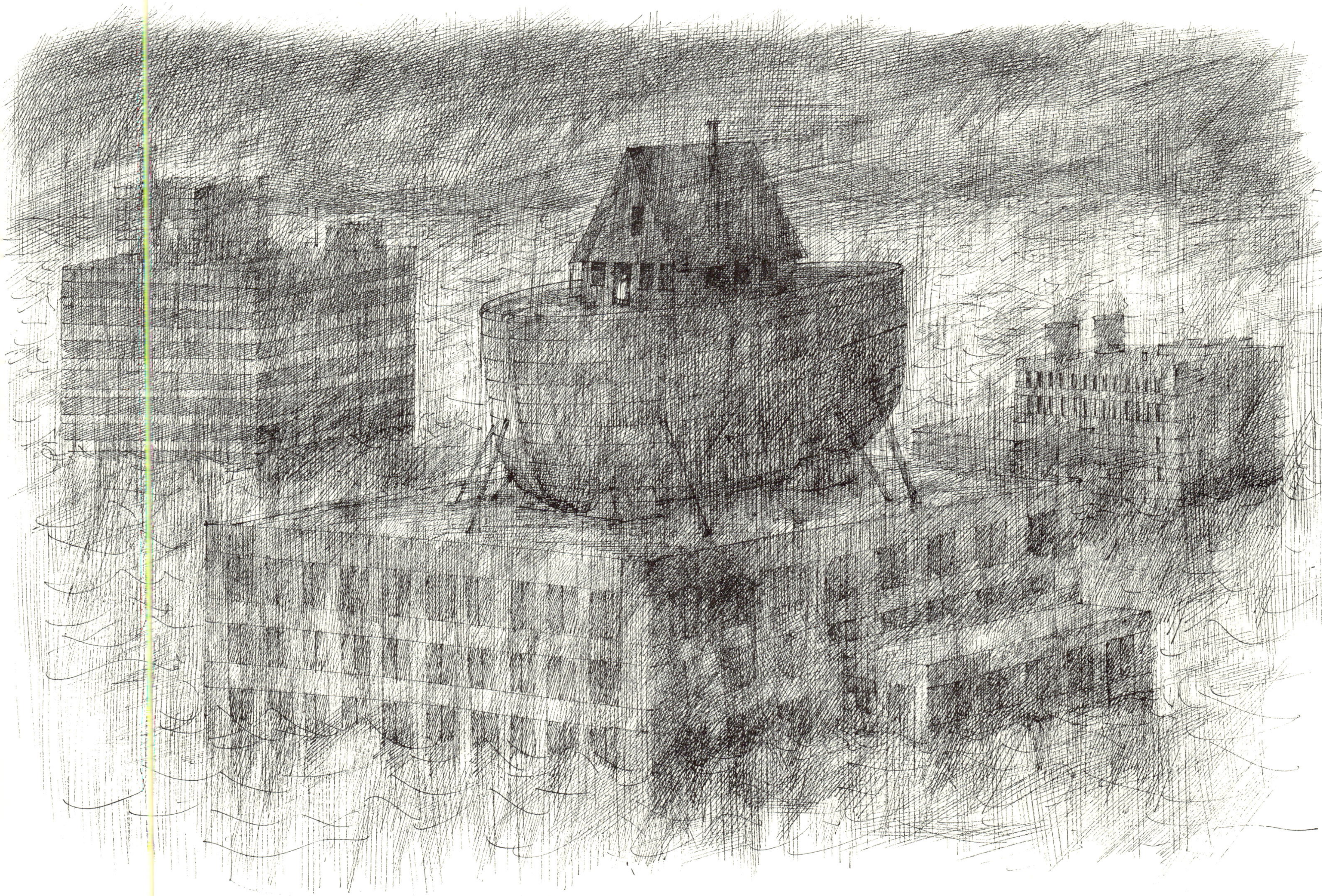

THE DELUGE. 1974

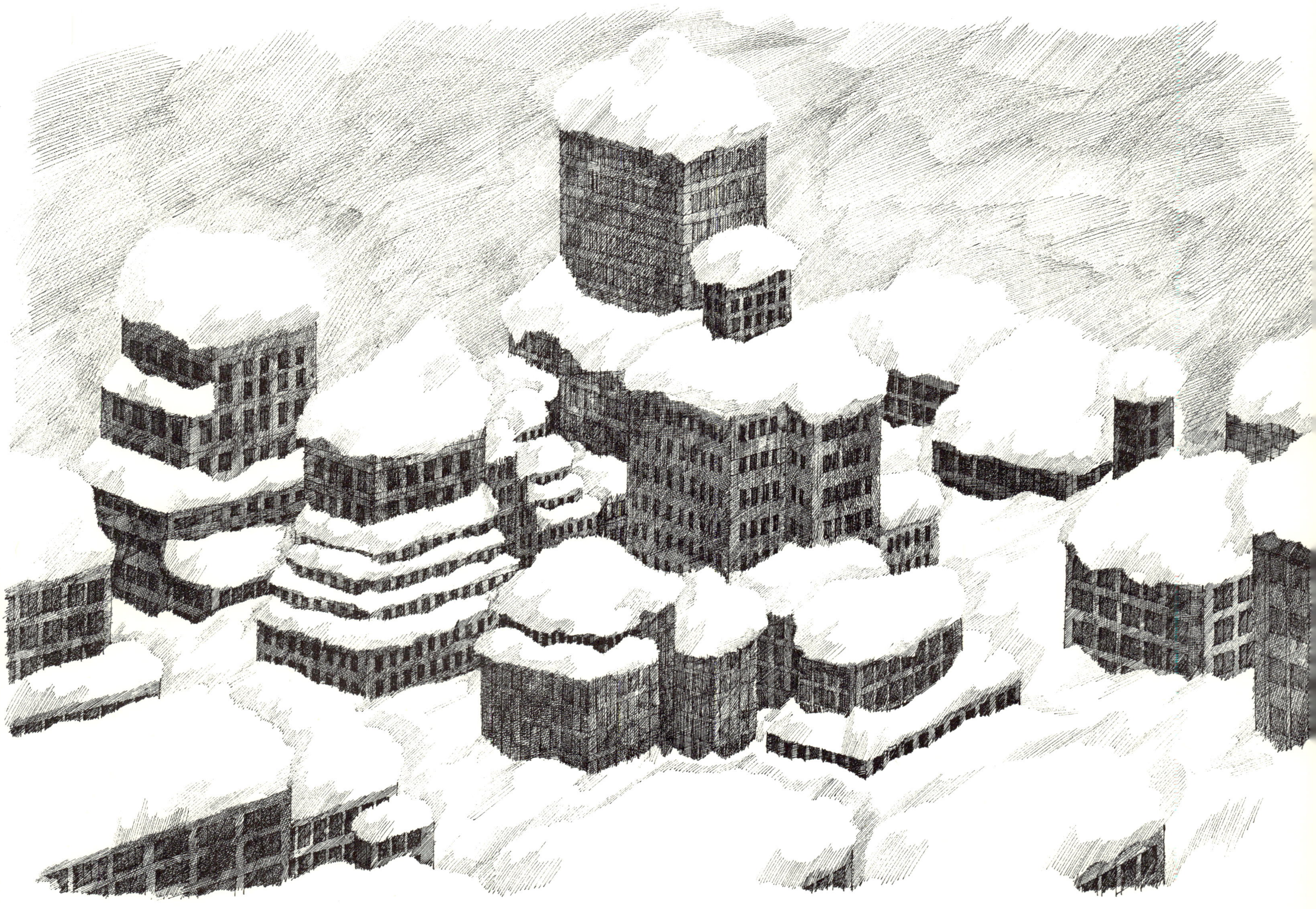

SNOWED-IN CITY. 1975

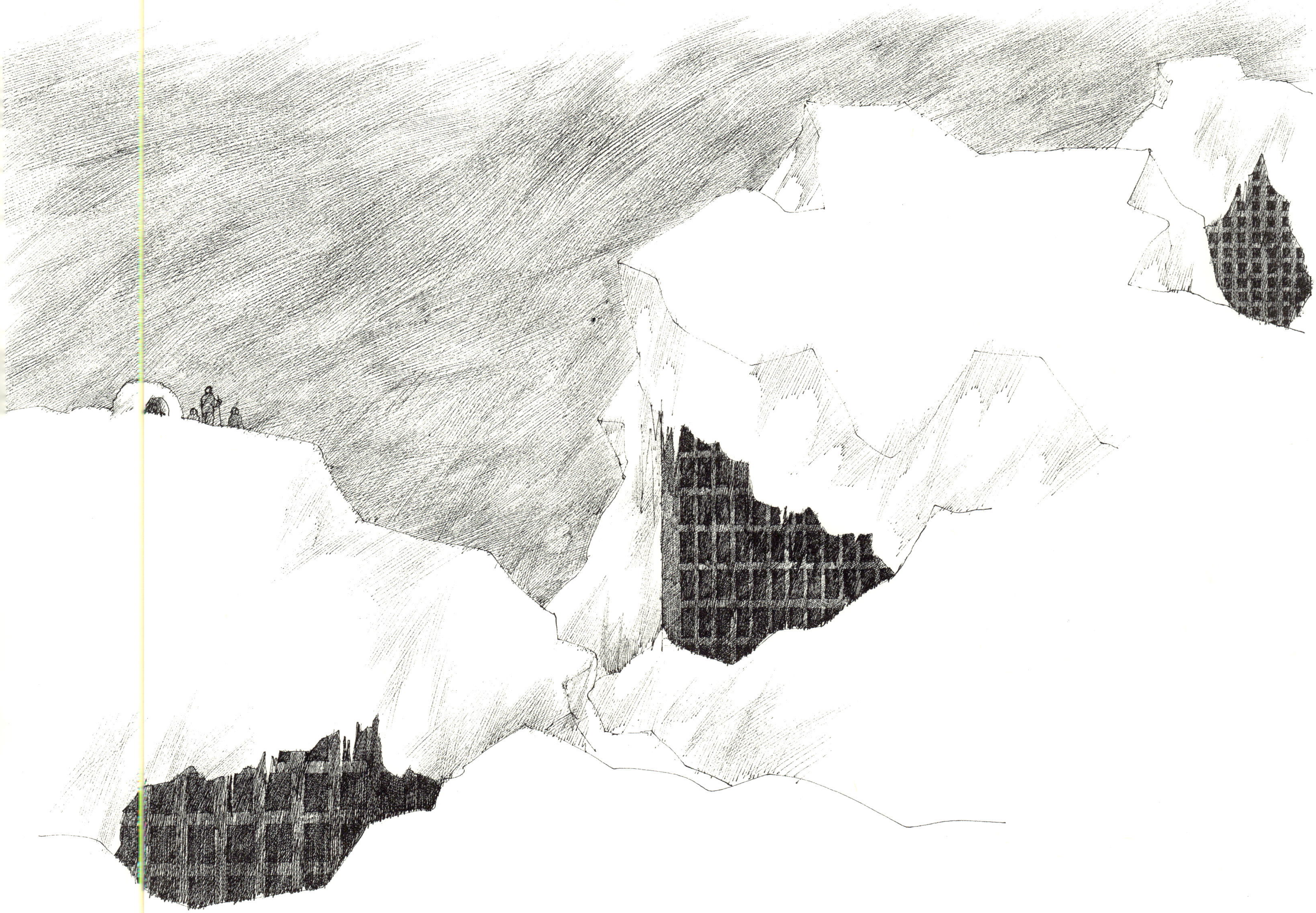

FROM THE LAST ICE AGE. 1976

6953 K